SA Tribes

*Who we are, how we live and what we want
from life in the new South Africa*

Errata

A gremlin crept in to the final edit on pages 48-49 of this print run!

Rural Survivalists (42.7%) are the largest group, comprising four tribes. They live traditional agrarian lifestyles in deep rural areas. They have the lowest level of human development and access to the formal sector.

Emerging Consumers (37.0%) includes five tribes. They have running water, electricity, and flush toilets and are beginning to add some luxuries - radios, TVs, fridge/freezers are among likely first choices.

Urban Middle Classes (12.5%) is not a middle class comparable to industrialised Western countries. Has many amenities associated with middle level human development, such as electricity, running water, common household appliances and motor cars.

Urban Elite (7.8%) includes three tribes and is the smallest and most advantaged group. Sophisticated, exposed to global culture and development, digitally-connected and active.

The sizes of the individual tribes given in Chapter 4 are correct as printed.

SA Tribes

*Who we are, how we live and what we want
from life in the new South Africa*

Steven M. Burgess

*with contributions from
Mari Harris
Professor Robert Mattes*

First published in 2002 in Southern Africa by
David Philip Publishers, an imprint of New Africa Books (Pty) Ltd,
99 Garfield Road, Claremont 7700, South Africa

© 2002 Steven M. Burgess

ISBN 0-86486-598-8

All rights reserved. No part of this publication may be reproduced,
stored in a retrieval system, or transmitted in any form or by any means,
electronic, mechanical, photocopying, recording or otherwise,
without the prior written permission of the publishers.

Design and typesetting by Christabel Hardacre
Printed and bound by ABC Press, Epping, South Africa

Dedication

To Colleen – with love and appreciation.

To little Thandiwe Bahia Burgess, my daughter. May God bless your bright mind and special soul. You are truly beloved.

To Ariel, Alethe, Richard and Jonathan, my other children. May God bless every step that you take and may you learn in your lives to treasure the great diversity of all people.

The author

Professor Steve Burgess is Research Director and Professor of Business Administration in Marketing at the Graduate School of Business, University of Cape Town. He was previously the Association of Marketers Professor of Marketing in the School of Economic and Business Studies, University of the Witwatersrand, where he completed his doctorate in 1990. He won the International Alumni Award from the Fisher College of Business at the Ohio State University in 1999, for service to the American and South African business community. He also chaired the marketing strategy track of the Academy of Marketing Science annual conference in 2000.

Professor Burgess has also enjoyed a distinguished business career and consults to a number of blue-chip South African, American and UK firms. He has been the Managing Director of Autopage Cellular (Pty) Ltd and Consumadata; Chairman of the South African Cellular Service Providers Association and a senior marketing executive with Johnson & Johnson South Africa, where he won numerous awards. He is a member of the editorial review board of the *International Journal of Advertising* and *Advances in Consumer Research* and has published numerous articles in journals such as *International Journal of Research in Marketing*, *Advances in Consumer Research*, *Journal of Cross-Cultural Psychology*, *South African Journal of Psychology* and *South African Journal of Business Management*. His research concerns change and stability in consumers and its impact on marketing strategy. He is a fellow of the Academy of Marketing Science and the International Trade Institute of Southern Africa and maintains membership in a number of local and international marketing associations.

The contributors

Mari Harris is a Director at Markinor (Pty) Ltd, one of South Africa's leading market research companies. Mari is a well-known and widely recognised political analyst and researcher. She holds three degrees, a BA in Communication Studies, a BA Honours in International Politics and an MA in International Politics from the University of Potchefstroom. Mari completed the Marketing Management course at the University of the Witwatersrand in July 1989. She joined Markinor in January 1989 as a Senior Research Executive, and was promoted to Account Director in December 1992 and Director in January 1997. She previously held research and consultancy positions at the Institute for Political and Africa Studies at the University of Potchefstroom and Strategic Concepts (Pty) Ltd, a socio-economic and political consultancy. She is a member of SAMRA (Southern African Marketing Research Association), WAPOR (World Association for Public Opinion Research) and ESOMAR (European Society for Opinion and Marketing Research). She has presented numerous papers at national and international conferences, with the focus mainly on public opinion issues.

Professor Robert Mattes is Associate Professor in the Department of Political Studies, University of Cape Town, and Director of the Democracy in Africa Research Unit in the new Centre for Social Science Research. Along with E. Gyimah-Boadi and Michael Bratton, he is co-founder and co-director of the Afrobarometer, a regular survey of Africans' attitudes toward democracy, markets and civil society. His recent work on voting behaviour, public opinion, and political culture and democratic consolidation in South Africa and Africa has appeared in the *British Journal of Political Science*, *Journal of Democracy and Democratization*. He holds a Ph.D. from the University of Illinois, Urbana-Champaign.

Contents

Chapter 1: Living in the new South Africa   1
Who we are, how we live, what we want

Chapter 2: Understanding our identity   10
What it is and how it affects our behaviour

Chapter 3: Introducing the tribes   35
Who they are and how they were identified

Chapter 4: Tribes of the new South Africa   51
The tribes profiled in detail

Chapter 5: Consumer behaviour   70
How you do the washing says a lot about who you think you are

Chapter 6: Uniquely African?   82
(by Robert Mattes)
What South Africa can learn from the rest of the continent

Chapter 7: One South African, one vote   98
(by Steve Burgess and Mari Harris)
Is democracy working and do we care?

Chapter 8: Closing thoughts   113
How to live happily ever after

Acknowledgements

First and foremost, we thank the nearly 15,000 South Africans who have participated as respondents in this project, the SA Tribes research programme.

SA Tribes has benefited from the comments of many blind reviewers, thanks to articles published in journals such as *International Journal of Research in Marketing*, *Journal of Cross-Cultural Psychology*, *Advances in Consumer Research* and *South African Journal of Business Management*. It has also profited from conferences hosted by the Academy of Marketing Science, Association for Consumer Research and the William Davidson Institute at the University of Michigan Business School and the Fisher College of Business at the Ohio State University.

I am grateful to my principal co-conspirator, Mari Harris, for her sharp wit, wise counsel and unfailing encouragement and support. We were very fortunate to have the constant support of Markinor's entire board of directors. We also thank Markinor's previous Managing Director, Sue Grant, for her challenge to 'do it' and her unwavering support.

We originally set out to chronicle the values of South Africans. I'm not sure that we would have expanded to address the more holistic concept of identity had it not been for a conversation I had with Alheit du Toit of Rand Water. Alheit shared a few obscure papers on social identity that I had not seen. I thank him here for that early support.

If this book was born in the Johannesburg offices of Markinor and the University of the Witwatersrand, then it was conceived during a dinner in Israel with my long-time friend and colleague Shalom Schwartz, the Leon and Clara Sznajderman Professor of Psychology at the Hebrew University in Jerusalem. Shalom is considered by many experts to be the world's leading authority on human values. He allowed us to use the *Portraits Values Questionnaire*, a new values survey intended for use in research environments such as South Africa. This book would never have happened without a reliable method of measuring values across all South Africans; that would not have been possible, in my opinion, without the use of Shalom's new survey.

I became a professor, consumer behaviourist and researcher as a result of the friendship and influence of Roger Blackwell, my long-time mentor, colleague, friend and 'older brother'. Roger encouraged me and allowed me to use his home as a base for research in the USA. I get great pleasure from our collaborations, one of which was published in *South African Journal of Business Management*. Roger and his beloved Tina know how much they mean to Colleen, the kids and me. No one has influenced my thinking and direction in life more than Roger and I am grateful.

I have benefited from my relationship with my alma mater, the Fisher College of Business at the Ohio State University. South African Michael Browne, now a professor of statistics and psychology at Ohio State, has also extended me great kindness, friendship and constant support over the years, for which I am grateful. I also thank Marilynn Brewer for discussing the implications of my findings with me on a few occasions and for her kindness and support. I am especially indebted to the Fisher College of Business. Various stints at Ohio State, including a visiting professorship in 2000 and almost annual research jaunts, sharpened my thinking and gave me access to one of the world's top business school faculties and information resources. Dean Joe Alutto, Bob Burnkrant, Cheryl Ryan, Steve Hills, Greg Allenby, Glenn Milligan, Martha Cooper, Curt Haugtvedt, Neeli Bendapudi, Bob Leone, Jim Ginter and everyone else at Fisher have always shared their time generously and I am much in their debt.

Rajeev Batra, Brent Chrite and Jan Svejnar of the University of Michigan Business School's William Davidson Institute have been very supportive. When a Top 5 business school such as Michigan says that emerging markets are important, the academic world sits up and listens. I truly appreciate being a WDI Faculty Affiliate and constantly gain from the interaction. This project especially benefited from the comments of researchers attending the conference held at the WDI, on marketing in transitional economies, at which my collaborator and colleague Jan-Benedict E. M. Steenkamp presented our initial findings of the SA Tribes project. Rajeev organised that conference, and produced and edited a book of papers that became the first of its kind on marketing issues in transitional economies. It is an historic contribution and I hope Rajeev will continue with future volumes.

I would also like to thank Michael Bond and Kwok Leung, both then at the Chinese University of Hong Kong, for inviting me to participate in the social axioms project, which allowed me to contextualise more effectively our work in values and personality traits.

Professor Jan-Benedict E. M. Steenkamp, the CentER Research Professor of Marketing and GfK Professor of Marketing at Tilburg University in the Netherlands, is the person who has most influenced my thinking about research in recent years. I will not embarrass him by writing about his personal qualities, except to say that he may be the most intelligent person I ever met and that I think of him with great respect and affection. He is well known for the high standard of his contributions to the very best scholarly marketing and psychology publications. I hate the fact that he writes better in English than I do, despite speaking Dutch as his home language! His invitation to take part in a special session on social identity at the Association for Consumer Research conference led to an on-going conversation that crystallised my thinking about how the components of social identity (values, personality traits, and observable characteristics) influence the process of consumer identification with products and services in emerging economies. The methodological excellence that characterises his regular articles in the top international marketing and psychology journals is an inspiration to researchers worldwide. I am honoured that he has been such an untiring supporter, colleague, collaborator and friend.

Professor Nick Segal, the Graduate School of Business (GSB) Director at the University of Cape Town, has made it possible for me to concentrate on SA Tribes by creating a place and culture where people who want to do research can get on with it. Our core and visiting faculty and our challenging MBA students have made comments that have sharpened my thinking or improved my viewpoint about the project. Frank Horwitz, Amy Marks, Janine Everson, Eric Wood, Kurt April, Nikki Weakley and Erin Sullivan deserve special comment. At Wits, Roger Sinclair, Dimitri Kapelianis, Alan Ohannessian, Theo Dagliadakis and Jennifer Thompson deserve special thanks.

A word of thanks also to the Departmental Secretary at the GSB, Elsie Plumb. Elsie acts as personal assistant, secretary, event coordinator, presentation designer and all-around model of efficiency. Elsie makes the GSB a better educational institution every day and her work and cheery attitude are much appreciated by all. Elsie took over the final details of SA Tribes, the indexing and checking of references and the like, and I thank her for doing this difficult task for me. Any errors, however, remain my responsibility.

Finally, and most importantly, I am deeply indebted to my wife Colleen. This book was an ordeal for her. If only she had a rand for every time she walked Thandiwe out of my office with the words: 'Come Thandi, Daddy needs to finish his book.' For years she has put much of her own academic research and other interests on hold so that she could shoulder the family responsibilities and free me to finish this journey. This book would never have been completed without her support.

1: Living in the new South Africa
Who we are, how we live, what we want

Have you ever noticed what happens when two strangers enter a room? Almost immediately, a dance of symbolic interaction begins.[1] No music is required, just an exchange of practised glances in which each scans the other for meaning while pretending not to notice. Gender? Age? Accent? Hairstyle? A tattoo? Skirt length or turn of a cuff? Which symbols has she chosen to wear, such as brand names, jewellery or social messages? What do these symbols say? Is she secure in her abilities? Is she at peace with herself and others? How do others react to her? Which characteristics do we share? How do we differ? What does she want to achieve in the current situation? From such cues, each will assess the other's probable role and relative status in the current situation: their occupation, education and social attitudes. No one needs to signal the beginning of the dance; it happens automatically, within the span of a heartbeat and without conscious effort. By the time they are introduced formally, people will already have reached a detailed 'first impression' of one another and chosen the way in which they will interact.

Even if it does sometimes lead to human folly, a substantial body of research suggests this dance of symbolic interaction is human nature. People search for identity cues in order to categorise others and choose how to interact with them, sometimes even when they think they know the other person quite well but observe something that does not match their previous categorisation of that person.[2] It is in such subtle details that we give the world clues about who we are, how we live and what we want from life.

Identity can be observed in the social categories people construct in everyday conversation. At the more aggregated levels of society, social categories of people come into play when politicians refer to 'constituencies' and 'special interest groups'; executives focus on 'target market segments', 'heavy-users' and 'different economic strata'; religious leaders speak to 'the faithful' and human rights organisations speak about 'the homeless' and 'the disadvantaged'. All such groups can be traced to relative similarities at some personal level: wealth, education, religion, gender, culture, beliefs, social attitudes, personal value importance, home language, occupation, geographic proximity, neighbourhood, nationality and other elements of social identity. All of these characteristics have the potential to be elements of social identity, to the extent that such characteristics or their influence on behaviour can be observed.

Whether human nature or human folly, social categorisation has fuelled a healthy debate in a rapidly changing South Africa. Actually, it isn't the act of categorising people into groups that's being debated. After all, anthropology and sociology almost exclusively study behaviour at the level of groups and psychology and economics devote much of their attention to the same level of social aggregation. No, the problem isn't the grouping of others – it's the definitions people use to group them. More specifically, it's the assumptions people make about others from different Apartheid racial groups.

The SA Tribes research programme

SA Tribes began as a study to help companies understand how South Africans were changing and what the commercial implications of that change were. Certain things were obvious from the inception of the study. Its scientific integrity would be of utmost importance. It would have to have a strong theoretical basis rooted neither in East nor West. The research tools would have to be applicable in the most and least developed populations and in rural and urban areas. Illiteracy and innumeracy could not be barriers to participation. Advanced cross-cultural research techniques would have to be used, including rigorous translation and back-translation procedures, but the results would have to be easily understood by ordinary people. People would have to be interviewed in their homes by highly trained interviewers of the same social standing using their home language. Items such as living standard measures would have to be visually inspected to ensure accurate findings.

Over time, it became apparent that SA Tribes could contribute to a wider and more important conversation taking place in South Africa, a conversation perhaps best introduced through an analogy. Scientists estimate that the gravitational pull of dark matter – which comprises some 90% of the universe – holds the galaxies in place even if we cannot see it. Clearly, astronomers need to understand and measure something so pervasive and influential and yet so difficult to observe directly. So, too, ordinary South Africans need to identify their commonality, which far outweighs their differences, if they are to rise above the differences that have become artificially magnified over time by Apartheid-era propaganda. Former US President Bill Clinton recently captured such thinking in a Richard Dimbleby Lecture in London:[3]

'... Now most of us believe that no one has the absolute truth. Indeed, in our societies, the most religious among us sometimes feel that most strongly, because we believe as children of God we are, by definition, limited in this life, in this body, with our minds. That life is a journey toward truth, that we have something to learn from each other, and that everybody ought to have a chance to make that journey. So for us, a community is just made up of anybody that accepts the rules of the game, everybody counts, everybody has a role to play, everybody deserves a chance and we all do better when we work together. Now, that's what this is about.

'This is not complicated. The people that want to kill us over our differences do so because they think their life doesn't matter except insofar as they are different from and better than others. Those of us who are trying to change ourselves and change them, we think our common humanity is more important and if we could just live up to its potential, the world would be a better place. And which side wins will shape the 21st century. What do you think is more important? The answer is easy to give, but very, very hard to live ... Think about how important your differences are to you. Think about how we all organize our lives in little boxes: man, woman, British, American, Muslim, Christian, Jew ... you know, everything in the world ... Think about everything you define yourself by. Our little boxes are important to us. And indeed, it is necessary. How could you navigate life if you didn't know the difference between the child and an adult, an African and an Indian, a scientist and a lawyer? We have to organize them, but somewhere along the way we finally come to understand that our life is more important than all these boxes we are in. And if we can't reach beyond that, we'll never have a fuller life. And the fanatics of the world, they love their boxes and they hate yours ...

'So, that's what I want you to think about. It's great that your kids will live to be 90 years old but I don't want it to be behind barbed wire. It's great that we're gonna have all these benefits of the modern world, but I don't want you to feel like you're emotional prisoners. And I don't want you to look at people who look different from you and see a potential enemy instead of a fellow traveller. We can make the world of our dreams for our children, but since it's a world without walls, it will have to be a home for all of our children.'

Such thinking suggests why serious researchers in South Africa work so hard to obtain representative samples and interrogate their research instruments for Western or African cultural assumptions, ideological rhetoric, simplistic characterisations, favoured theories and unsubstantiated opinions – and SA Tribes could be no different. Only in this way could the data provided by the respondents present the portraits and content of different types of South Africans in a way that could be easily understood. If the final result were to be successful, it would have to have substantial intuitive appeal to ordinary South Africans. It would have to allow them to understand the implications of each social identity group: its needs and preferences, its commonality and uniqueness in the warp and woof of South African society.

Social identity

Although we measure a holistic range of identity characteristics, we focus most on the concept of social identity in SA Tribes. Social identity is a well-established concept that emerged in the social psychology research literature, driven mainly by the French psychologist Henri Tajfel.[4] It is an amalgam comprised of the observable characteristics of a person, their values, lifestyle and social attitudes. The choice of social identity as the fundamental characteristic for the SA Tribes research emerged naturally from my research into change and stability of consumers. Since the mid-1980s, I have been focusing on the value priorities and personality traits of South Africans and the influence of values and traits on consumer behaviour. Values and personality traits are two of the three major components of social identity (the third being observable demographic characteristics).

The most recent research results reported in SA Tribes are derived from interviews conducted in the final quarter of 2001. However, we began to explore the major human characteristics known to be related to social identity in 1997. This book reports mainly on three waves of research, during which approximately 10,500 South Africans were interviewed in their homes by Markinor, a leading South African marketing research house affiliated to Gallup International and to Walker Research International. In addition, graduate students completing research in the Graduate School of Business at the University of Cape Town and in the School of Economic and Business Sciences at the University of the Witwatersrand have assisted me in data collection. I am thankful to them and our corporate sponsors who have supported their studies. Throughout, we have tried to collect data in as reliable and as valid a way as possible, choose the most appropriate data analyses and allow those data to 'do the talking'. We provide extensive information about the reliability, validity and cross-cultural measurement invariance in academic papers to which we refer in text. We have paid particular attention to cross-cultural measurement invariance, which is especially important and too often ignored in South African research.

During the course of classroom or seminar discussions, I have often been asked why SA Tribes focuses on social identity when so much of the contemporary debate in South Africa concerns racial identity, especially Apartheid racial identity? Conversely, I am asked why I include racial identity at all. Of course, one could point to the results of human genetics research, which thoroughly discredits the notion of a pure race. It is hard to read genetics research findings, and I include the human genome project, without concluding that we are one human family sharing incredible genetic similarity. This does not disprove the notion of perceived racial identity, which is very real to people who perceive it, or suggest that racial identity does not influence behaviour in South Africa.

Trevor Manuel recently told a UCT Graduate School of Business Annual Dinner that: 'Apartheid may be dead but its corpse is still very much with us' in the separate opportunities and experiences of life in different 'race groups' under Apartheid – in the family, neighbourhood, church, school, sporting club and workplace. Let us be perfectly clear about this, without disregarding recent advances, people of different races continue to lead essentially separate lives in South Africa. Race continues to be correlated to differences in education, occupation, household income, infant mortality, threat of social violence, malnutrition, access to human development and a host of other social indicators of wealth and development. An artificial sense of racial identity, reinforced by this pernicious legacy of unequal opportunity, is Apartheid's most spoiled fruit. Ignoring racial identity removes it from the analysis and precludes the intelligent assessment of just how important it remains. Moreover, research shows that ignoring racial identity can have very negative and unintended consequences, among which is the accentuation of perceived differences as individuals 'defend' their perceived identity. This suggests that South Africans risk far more in ignoring racial identities that were manufactured and reinforced during more than 100 years of separate development than by recognising their influence (I return to this in the next chapter).

Although racial identity has influence, there is no evidence to suggest that it is a prepotent influence on behaviour. In fact, there is much evidence to suggest that racial identity is a very weak influence on behaviour in most situations, even in a country where it was artificially exaggerated by one of the most powerful social engineering and propaganda campaigns in human history. Ask yourself which identity a crying baby is likely to evoke: parental identity or racial identity? Which identity is a discussion about buying a laptop computer likely to evoke: occupational identity or racial identity? Clearly, there is an opportunity to develop alternative ways of thinking about similarities and differences in South Africans that pass the test of daily interactions. We believe that way is to think of their many social identities.

Advantages of social identity theory

Thinking of people as having complex social identities offers theoretical, conceptual and practical advantages over thinking of them as members of racial identity groups. From a theoretical standpoint, social identity and its influences have been well described in the scientific literature, in more and less developed countries. Research has consistently shown that identity is complex, that people are aware of many social identities and that these identities act as a unifying and predictable influence on their behaviour. Moreover, it is widely accepted that people choose an appropriate identity from what has been called a 'digest of selves'[5] (namely father, son, Muslim, football fan, brother, lover, colleague, friend) in response to situational cues and often without conscious thought.

Conceptually, social identity is isomorphic to the human condition in South Africa. It allows one to conceive of the varied influences and complexity of changing individual characteristics, social interaction patterns and associations, diverse environmental influences and varied living circumstances. It is compatible with most major approaches to understanding human behaviour. It can be reconciled with the major tenets of psychodynamic, trait-factor, humanist and behaviouralist theories. It allows for stability and change, personal growth and decline, and the influence of personal, social and environmental forces people encounter in life without prescribing the relative influence of any of these forces.

On a practical level, individuals and organisations can apply an understanding of social identity in daily life. The holistic generalised portraits that emerge from social identity research are easily understood and applied without being prescriptive, because it is understood that personal, social and environmental forces that are active within a particular situation activate the influence of various identities. People gain an opportunity to understand their essential commonality with others and to appreciate differences in characteristics that underlie different worldviews, values, attitudes and behaviours. Thus, large general portraits, such as are presented in *SA Tribes*, are understood to describe underlying general patterns of influence. Because people may take on and cast away various social identifications (woman, wife, mother, widow) during life, for relatively long or momentary periods, organisations can focus on understanding the particular influence of various identifications and the life events that mark their arrival (leaving home, marriage, giving birth, death of a spouse). On the other hand, it allows researchers and policymakers to consider highly detailed identifications by individuals within specific situations, whether their interest is derived from responsibilities in a commercial, social welfare, political, religious or any other kind of organisation. Basing one's understanding of others on their social identity avoids the presumption that people are limited to membership of a few simplistic groups and unable to change. Rather, it assumes that people have many different identities, which are activated by situational cues and then become influential. This allows for detailed strategies to be developed. Moreover, it allows organisations to train staff responsible for implementing strategies so that they can identify the needs of the people they serve more accurately and bring much deeper empathy to bear in their interactions with them.

Emerging economies and transitional societies

The next chapter reviews the recent strides made in understanding social identity and how it influences people and their behaviour. It will show that a body of research worldwide has established the influence of social identity. We know that people compare the world around them to what they know and that, as part of this process of cognition, they perhaps automatically categorise people into various social groups based on their previous knowledge of different 'types' of people and what they glean from the sensory cues they observe. The process allows people to act more smoothly and effectively as social beings because it allows them to predict how others will act in response to certain situations and behaviours. There's a certain order to life and it's the way 'we' and 'they' 'always have been' or 'are supposed to be'.

This is all very neat and tidy. Hundreds of studies in relatively stable societies suggest that it leads to very predictive theories about how people will behave within certain situations. Nevertheless, we don't know very much about social identity and its effect on behaviour in rapidly changing societies.

There are two kinds of rapidly changing societies in the world today. *Emerging economies* are countries that are undergoing rapid economic development. The globalisation of trade, information and computing has stimulated incredible pockets of economic growth in these countries, and in some cases, full emergence to the levels of human development witnessed in the most industrialised countries. People residing in *transitional societies* may experience economic change, but the main factor that distinguishes these countries is a changing socio-political order. The rapid changes taking place in the transitional societies of the former Soviet Union and Eastern Bloc countries, the encouragement of private enterprise in China, and the global movement toward democracy have fuelled incredible social changes and tensions in many countries.

South Africa is not unique but it is one of a few countries that can be categorised as both an *emerging economy* and a *transitional society*. This need not be a disadvantage. To the contrary, it can be seen as a renewable source of global competitiveness. Consider that six out of every ten people on our planet reside in the 25 emerging economies regularly monitored by *The Economist* magazine. While these countries do have their special problems and higher risk profiles, they are generally growing at twice the pace of the industrialised West. Their populations are young and possess growing household spending power. Most importantly, they are undergoing a rapid pace of change that is unique in human history. Never before have so many people moved from the peasantry to full-blown consumer societies in such a short space of time. South African business experienced not only the change but also the on-going transition.

This is taking its toll around the world. Talk in boardrooms, government chambers and university halls is beginning to recognise the need to understand how rapid change impacts on social identity, social categorisation and intergroup behaviour. Organisations are finding that their very survival can be threatened overnight by discontinuous innovations. Executives working at the boundaries of organisations (marketing, sales and customer service) must be particularly adept at sensing and responding to the rapid pace of change.

As demographic ageing and market saturation slow product sales in Western industrialised economies, interest in the emerging economies is growing – so much so that the United States has identified the ten most attractive markets out of which the majority of its export sales growth will come in this century (South Africa is one of the ten). The rationale of selling people their first TV set, instead of their third, is easily understood. Firms from the wealthiest nations have been investing much more heavily into the emerging economies. They have found that they need new skills to conduct business in the duality they have encountered. It is a duality that most South Africans understand very well: rich and poor, rural and urban, historically advantaged and disadvantaged. It is one that academic and applied researchers in the industrialised West believe that their countries need to understand better.[6]

About this book

This book is organised in the following way. The next chapter introduces the social identity concept, briefly reviews key findings that have emerged from social identity research and discusses the implications for understanding consumer behaviour and social attitudes in a transitional society such as South Africa. Chapters 3 and 4 present the 16 tribes and group them into four larger clusters. Subsequent chapters present a more detailed textual portrait for each of the 16. We identify their values, personality traits, geo-demographic characteristics, living standards and participation in the formal financial sector and various product categories. After linking social identity to differences in product category participation and living standards, we demonstrate the usefulness of social identity in explaining softer issues such as activities, interests, opinions and brand preference.

Our journey is aided greatly by chapter contributions from Mari Harris, who shares some of her findings concerning the political opinions and attitudes of the SA Tribes in a co-authored chapter. My University of Cape Town colleague, Professor Bob Mattes, reports on social identity in 11 African countries, as measured by the Afrobarometer© study of political and economic attitudes toward democracy.

Summary

It is hard to think of an aspect of human behaviour that could not be understood better if one understood the social identity of the people being studied. We are pleased to be able to demonstrate how social identity can be used to explain a wide range of commercial, social and political attitudes and behaviours and we could have put forward many more examples from our research if space permitted. We hope that you will draw on the content of this book to improve your understanding of the people who interest you and that you will enjoy the journey of exploration as much as we have.

2: Understanding our identity
What it is and how it affects our behaviour

> 'Almost cut my hair, it happened just the other day, it's getting
> 'kinda long, I guess I could've said it wasn't my way, but I didn't and
> I wonder why, I feel like lettin' my freak flag fly, yes I feel like I owe
> it to someone ...'
>
> David Crosby, *Almost Cut My Hair*, 1969

It's been a generation since Crosby, Stills, Nash & Young vocalised the Woodstock generation's identity but if you watch American baby-boomers shop for music, they're ignoring the latest hits to continue their romance with the music that charged the air at Yasgur's Farm.[1] Many radio DJs are playing hits by artists such as *The Beatles, The Supremes, Eagles, The Rolling Stones, Led Zeppelin* or *The Temptations* more often today than ever. Rock concert popularity in 2002 testifies to a near retirement age generation that intends to 'rock-on' until it reaches the grave. *Aerosmith, Crosby, Stills, Nash & Young, Elton John, Billy Joel, Bob Dylan* and *The Moody Blues* are unbelievably back in the Top Ten![2] The hippie years resonate with many South Africans as well; *Rabbitt* albums remain hot property decades after their release. What is it that burns teenage music preferences, favourite sports teams, political party affiliations or brand names so deeply into our hearts, minds and souls? Why do people *identify* so strongly with these relics of their teenage years?

SA Tribes proposes that the answer lies in whom we think we are, how we live and what we want from life; in other words, our identity.

What is identity?

Who are you? Perhaps the better question is: 'Who are you now?' People have many identities; they call upon them for aid in directing behaviour depending on the situation at hand.[3] Who are *you* now? Are you father, brother, Christian, soccer fan? Mother, manager, lover, daughter?

Think about it for a moment and you'll agree that, although everyone knows what 'father' means, each of us has a network of unique associations with the word. To one person, father may mean 'strong', to another 'caring' and to yet another 'conservative'. We all construct networks of related concepts, called schemas,[4] in which we associate the meaning for such words.

Identity is constructed in a similar way. As people encounter personal, social and situational forces in life, they learn more about their identity. They use this information to construct three different types of schemas about themselves: a personal identity, a relational identity and a social identity.[5] These different identities represent different identification processes and, within a particular situation, any or all of these identity types may be activated.

Personal identity

Personal identity is learned through introspection and experience as one considers 'what I sense', 'how I feel' and 'what I think'. When it is activated, people act in their self-interest. When a situation activates your personal identity, you become oriented to yourself primarily as an individual, thinking of your personal value priorities, goals and personality traits. You are motivated by self-interest and personal preferences. This, by the way, does not imply a negative, narcissistic image of the self but rather a frame of reference in which you are motivated by self-reward and in which you compare yourself to others on a one-to-one basis.

Relational identity

However, contrary to what your economics professor probably told you, people do not always act in their self-interest. Much of what one learns about identity is learned from, or substantially influenced by, others. From early childhood, we observe that people often define themselves in relation to others, taking on different roles and statuses.[6] When relational identity is activated, people evaluate themselves in relation to responsibilities and social requirements that benefit others.

Sue is a physiotherapist. When her relational identity is activated, she is motivated primarily to think of her identity as one who seeks benefits and rewards for others. She may think of herself as a healer or caregiver, as an efficient employee or effective colleague at work, or as a friend at a time when another is in need. Thus, she is likely to evaluate herself and her behaviour by paying careful attention to fulfilling the demands of her role relationship to others.

Social identity

Sue's social identities are a third collection of beliefs individuals hold about 'who I am'. We all learn about various 'we's' and 'they's' in this world and that 'people' expect 'people like us' to behave in certain ways and 'people like them' to behave differently. Sue's identity as a physiotherapist, medical professional, human-rights activist and Anglican may cause her to think of herself as a person who represents a group of people, and to evaluate 'her group' versus other groups. Sue may define her social identity group broadly or narrowly. For instance, her identity as an Anglican influences her to go to church on Sunday. Her identity as a member of a four-person team working the night shift at a local hospital may influence her perceptions and behaviour toward hospital administration. In whatever way she defines her identity in a particular situation, social identity is the part of her identity derived from knowing that she is a member of a social group or groups and the emotional significance she attaches to that membership.[7]

The notion of group identity remains a sensitive issue in South Africa because of the imposed racial group identities of Apartheid.[8] To this day, many people remain very conscious of Apartheid group identity. It's a troubling issue that causes many South Africans to wonder if South Africa will ever truly leave its Apartheid legacy behind. However, race is only one element of social identity. While standing in a queue at the bank, Sue may recognise her identity as a university graduate, woman, competent investor, mother or bank customer. Any or all of these identities may become influential. Thus any characteristic, even race in South Africa, may be irrelevant in determining the social identities that will influence behaviour in a particular situation.

The role of social identity in South Africa

The SA Tribes project is based on the premise that identity is a very powerful influence on actions such as voting, product or brand choice, media consumption or investment behaviour. There is growing international recognition that social identity theory may be especially helpful in understanding how change affects people in emerging economies and transitional societies. This is because the volatile socio-political and economic environment that characterises such countries can alter the desirability of group membership, relax traditional boundaries that have defined groups and create opportunities to move from group to group (i.e.

social mobility). These changes are happening at a pace unprecedented in human history, with people transiting from the peasantry to the boardroom in the span of a generation. As a result, new social interaction patterns, lifestyle experiences and consumption choices emerge that have important symbolic implications for the self-perceptions of all groups. The effect is significant and substantial, affecting the core elements of social identity: value priorities, personality traits and the meaning of observable characteristics.

SA Tribes proposes that *intergroup* behaviour (as opposed to *interpersonal* behaviour) could be much more likely to occur in South Africa, not only because it is the logical conclusion of a country trying to overcome a racially-divided past, but also because of the emerging and transitional nature of the country. This chapter sets out a brief overview of social identity theory and its structural components.[9] We begin by identifying the major assumptions of the theory and by differentiating interpersonal and intrapersonal behaviour. Next, we report some of SA Tribes' findings concerning value priorities and personality traits in South Africa. We end the chapter with a brief summary.

Social identity theory

The 1960s and 1970s was a period of prosperity and change in Western Europe and America. It was at this time in human history – so early in our understanding of globalism and its effects – that social identity theory was proposed and refined by French psychologist Henri Tajfel.[10] His thinking about intergroup and interpersonal behaviour continues to influence the way we think about human behaviour, and the way we understand the situations in which people are likely to act as individuals and those in which they are likely to act as members of groups.

Basic premises

Identity is constructed as part of a never-ending process influenced by personal, social and environmental forces. This results in a stable, but not fixed, sense of identity that influences behaviour in a reasonably predictable manner.[11] Identity does not only serve an ontological function – that is, it is not simply a receptacle into which people compile a summated image of who they are and who they want to be. Its construction serves a utilitarian function as well, because it causes people to enter an internal conversation in which prevailing values, attitudes and beliefs are compared as circumstances and situations change. This results in internal conflicts that must be resolved through internal dialogue and negotiation.[12]

Building on earlier work on personal identity,[13] Tajfel argued that people also define themselves at the level of social identity as part of this process. His major innovation was to draw attention to the possibility that any interaction with another person could be occurring on multiple levels: on one hand as a person-to-person interaction and, on the other hand, as an interaction of two people representing all or some of the groups to which they belong. This implied two types of identity to Tajfel. *Personal identity* includes all of the perceptions a person holds about 'who I am' in comparison to other individuals, and *social identity*, which refers to the perceptions a person holds about 'who I am' in my role as a member of an emotionally important social group or category. To Tajfel, then, social identity is a kind of depersonalised self-concept about 'people like us' that influences the way we interact with our environment and others.

Consider how personal, relational and social identities might impact on success in a contemporary South African communications problem: the perception of an advertisement encouraging safe sexual practices to prevent HIV/AIDS transmission. In the case of *personal identity*, the person sees oneself as an individual with unique characteristics. So, assuming that the ad is involving enough to engage his thought processes, he might consider the risk implied by his and his partner's sexual behaviour as compared to other individuals. Sexual practices aren't something that many people talk about freely, even with their closest friends, but he might be able to compare his behaviour with the few people that have confided in him. The advert may activate *relational identity*, causing him to think about how promiscuous behaviour on his part might expose others to harm. In the case of *social identity*, the person is seen as a depersonalised entity indicative of a class or type of individuals, such as males, South Africans, fathers, sportsmen, husbands or members of an occupation group. 'How should fathers react to this advert? What should responsible husbands do?'

Any aspect of the advertisement may cause him to recognise these aspects of his social identity and consider instead the sexual practices of 'people like us' and the implied risks. He may identify with the advertisement and be influenced positively. Alternatively, he may incorrectly conclude that HIV/AIDS is a risk only to people who are unlike him (sexually promiscuous, different sexual orientation, another race, etc.) and 'tune out' immediately. Either way, it is easy to see how personal, relational and social identity may enhance or inhibit the information processing and persuasion of the advertisement.

A positive social identity

From the perspective of social identity theory, these effects on a person's reactions to an advertisement may be explained – at least in part – by the universal desire people have to achieve and maintain a sense of positive social identity. According to social identity theory, individuals derive a feeling of positive social identity from belonging to desirable social groups; that is, from their affiliations to groups that they perceive to be positively distinctive from other groups. When a person feels a sense of positive identity, he associates himself with qualities that enable him to influence people and situations and at least partially control his environment. He will also feel that he compares favourably to others.[14] This has many implications of interest to policy makers. For instance, people may buy, use or dispose of products or choose political party affiliations in their efforts to pursue a positive social identity or to avoid negatively distinctive groups.

Products and services may also play a role when people find themselves in undesirable social identity groups. People in such circumstances can be thought of as pursuing three different strategies.[15] Consider the case of cigarette smokers – a group that has come under increasing social pressure in recent years. *Social mobility* refers to movement between groups. Quitting smoking allows people to move from the 'smoker' to the 'non-smoker' group. For social mobility strategies to be effective, group boundaries must be permeable. This is not always so. Many group boundaries are very rigid and mobility can be difficult. For example, many professions use examinations to determine who can and who cannot be admitted to groups. In some countries, one's tribe or caste may determine to which groups one can belong.

Perhaps aided and abetted by some of the most persuasive advertising ever conducted, many cigarette smokers have pursued *social creativity* strategies over the years. Social creativity strategies attempt to improve the desirability of membership of groups that are perceived as negative. In the 1950s, American cigarette ads frequently showed doctors and sports heroes enjoying a cigarette. Social creativity may emerge naturally as part of a social identity group's response to society or its environment. The 'black is beautiful' campaign of the American civil rights movement is a fantastic example of a social creativity strategy. However, social creativity sometimes is not enough and people feel the need to pursue a more aggressive strategy. *Social conflict* is a strategy that occurs when people actively challenge the desirability of groups and set out to overturn an existing or imposed order.

In-group bias

Personal, relational and social identities are distinct aspects of a total identity that may vary in complexity. Each identity type may operate independently and any or all may influence a particular behaviour within the context of a particular situation. When social identity is activated, intergroup behaviour occurs. *Intergroup behaviour* is distinguished by the biased treatment of in-groups and out-groups. Consequently, even when it is not true, people perceive the possibility that they will receive better treatment from other members of the in-group and worse treatment from those in the out-group.

The notion of in-groups (simply put, 'us') and out-groups ('them') was established long before Tajfel's seminal article on intergroup discrimination.[16] Nevertheless, working at a time when many countries were dealing with the immediate consequences of post-colonialism and American cities were burning with racial tension, Tajfel attracted much attention by linking social identity (and its emotional significance) to discrimination. He proposed that the need to strive for a positive social identity would result in prejudice, as the desire to affiliate with an in-group encourages the recruitment of an out-group that performs the role of a devalued contrast.[17]

Tajfel was interested in isolating the effects of group membership and designed an innovative research design, called the *minimal intergroup situation paradigm*,[18] in which people were placed in groups randomly and then differentiated into groups in a way that they could be said to differ only on their perceived group membership. For instance, selecting respondents for a study, randomly placing them in two groups and calling one group 'greens' and the other 'blues' would meet Tajfel's design requirements.

Possibly the most striking and consistent finding of social identity research concerns *bias toward the in-group*. Perhaps to assist themselves in their efforts to attain or maintain positive social identity, people treat in-groups more favourably than out-groups.[19] They report that they like people from their in-group more. They evaluate the in-group more favourably and are biased in their behaviour toward them and judgements of them. These findings of bias toward the in-group have emerged consistently over three decades in just about any region of the world one can imagine, even when groups are constructed on what could only be called the most flimsy and artificial of distinctions – such as 'greens' and 'blues'. In-group bias is especially interesting to marketers because it extends to things that people associate with the in-group,[20] such as products, brands or political parties. Thus, products perceived to be for 'my group' are especially appealing. This may be because products designed for a particular social identity group fulfil their unique needs; it may also be because buying the product shows loyalty to the group.

Tajfel surmised that any symbols and group identifications indicated by a person's observable characteristics – such as their gender, hairstyle or attitude toward natural foods – could be sufficient to induce intergroup behaviour. Substantial research since has consistently supported his contention. Psychologists generally accept that intergroup behaviour is taking place whenever people belonging to a group interact individually or collectively with a person or persons from another group in terms of their group identifications.[21] Thus, when David Crosby sings about his 'freak flag', he sings about one such group identification. Long hair, bell-bottom jeans, wide belts, tie-dyed clothes, Vietnam War protests, social attitudes toward social equality and war, the peace sign and attitudes toward 'saving the environment' were all group identifications that had special meaning to boomers (generally positive) and their American elders (generally negative) a generation ago. The lack of television, or another globalised audiovisual medium, ensured that long hair and other identifications of the Woodstock generation would have at least a somewhat different meaning on South African university campuses, but much shared meaning did travel across the cultures. For instance, the Vietnam War did not affect many South Africans directly but another 'War in Nam' did have meaning and did attract protests, albeit much more subdued. For many South Africans, especially those in rural areas, the symbols of the Woodstock generation communicated very little of that shared meaning.

Bias toward the in-group may indeed suggest some negative consequences of out-group formation, but it does not necessarily suggest an aggressive response to others who are different. Out-groups can be distrusted, disparaged, and aggressively acted against but there is evidence that intergroup aggression may be due to other factors.[22] In fact, studies suggest that in-group-out-group bias is much more about favouring the in-group than disadvantaging the out-group. For instance, in-group bias has been shown to disappear if it means the out-group will be treated badly.

Many of the observations that have emerged from social identity research suggest special reasons for considering its effects in South Africa. One reason is the consistent finding that people perceive members of in-groups and out-groups to be more similar to one another within their group (i.e. more homogeneous to other members of the group). Contact with members of other groups has been found to reduce such perceptions; working toward a common goal with members of other groups has been shown to reduce such perceptions even more effectively. Conversely, intergroup competition has been shown to heighten perceptions of group conflict and influence – leading to derogation of out-groups, negative stereotypes, prejudice and other undesirable outcomes. If perceptions of intragroup homogeneity are persistent, widely observed and highly relevant for understanding identity influences on post-Apartheid behaviour, then South Africans have very good reasons to understand the factors that stimulate people to assume social identities. Anyone in a position of major responsibility, in any organisation that interacts with the public, needs to understand what triggers intergroup behaviour.

Situation instigates intergroup behaviour

As noted earlier, intergroup behaviour occurs when one person in an interaction perceives the other as a member of a different group. Tajfel posited that social identity is most likely to be activated in situations that meet three criteria. First, the situation must cause the person to identify two or more clearly differentiated groups of people. Second, people within each group will believe that they are relatively more similar to one another than they are to those of the other group on at least one distinguishing characteristic. Third, the groups must be reasonably expected to behave in a meaningfully different way.

Awareness of differentiated group

People commonly recognise many in-groups in a particular situation. Intergroup behaviour is more likely when the differences between groups are so meaningful that a person perceives in-group and out-group relationships. This means that the mere perception of differentiated groups is insufficient to stimulate intergroup behaviour. People must become conscious of *meaningful* group differences in order to activate the influence of social identity – implying that the differentiating characteristic must evoke a normative influence (an influence to adhere to group expectations) in the context of the current situation. Considering the opening example of this chapter, David Crosby evoked a meaningful symbol in *Almost Cut My Hair* that was invested with meaning about group identity at that time. Cutting one's hair was visible evidence of 'copping out to the establishment' (i.e. adhering to the group norms of the out-group). It doesn't hold the same meaning for Boomers' children. It didn't hold the same meaning, and perhaps had no meaning at all, in the villages of rural KwaZulu-Natal at the time, where it may have evoked 'foreigner', 'Westerner' or simply 'not us'. It didn't even hold the same meaning on South African university campuses because television had not yet launched and there was no medium to communicate the full meaning of what it meant to be part of that group. Long hair eventually lost its meaning when Boomers found that the jobs they needed to survive required them to cut their hair.

People generally differentiate groups based on three main classes of human characteristics: values, personality traits and observable characteristics (such as age, race, gender, etc.).[23] Group identity may be perceived based on one or a combination of these characteristics. However, although people may perceive many characteristics, it is important to remember that group identity will only be based on characteristics to which meaning can be attributed. A person is more likely to perceive differences in others to be meaningful if he had a recent experience, or frequent experiences, with others who have that characteristic or if the attribute is chronically accessible in others. In South Africa, of course, race is one such characteristic that has been artificially accentuated for generations.

Perceived similarity

Research shows that people who identify with a group generally tend to exaggerate their similarity with other people in the group. The more meaningful the characteristics that people share with others in a group, the stronger the potential that exists for identification with the group and adherence to its norms and values. Physical appearance, which is linked to differences in race, gender and age, appears to be a primitive base upon which people categorise others. This suggests why race remains such a hot topic in South Africa. South Africa's Apartheid legacy is the perceived correspondence of similarities in education, access to resources, work experiences, living standards, culture and other social facts that can be linked to the physical similarity of racial categorisation, even if that correspondence may be in the process of erosion daily.

Behavioural differences

Finally, the groups must behave differently. This may imply only that the groups will behave differently by adopting goals, attitudes or beliefs or it may imply overt behaviour such as the adoption of certain products or brands. The specific behaviour isn't important. Rather, it is important that perceived group identity lead to different behaviours. This has a reinforcing effect on group identity by validating group expectations about appropriate behaviour.

Social identity as a perceptual lens

One winter day when I was an undergraduate at Ohio State, a person wearing a winter coat and hat walked slowly to the front of the lecture theatre gesticulating and complaining bitterly about a bad mark. Interrupting a lecture in front of some 700 students, the unknown person struck the professor in the face so hard it knocked him down and there was blood running from his mouth and nose. It was all over very quickly and the attacker left the venue, physically intimidating the one person who started to stand up to act in the defence of the professor. Two campus police officers detained the suspect immediately on leaving the lecture theatre. We could hear continued struggling and threats, as the person was subdued just outside the venue. One police officer ran into the class, asked us to sit down and not discuss what we had seen but to write it down immediately in case it was needed for evidence. We were eventually told the attack was not real, after our 'affidavits' had been collected for immediate analysis by a waiting statistical team. If the assailant had made good on the escape, the class would have focused the manhunt on an African-American male, weighing 80–85 kilograms and standing 175–180 cm tall. Less than 15 students correctly identified the attacker as a white woman less than 160 cm tall and weighing only about 50 kilograms. How could 95% of the people in such a large class be so wrong?

Benefits and costs of categorising others

Humans have a powerful social motive that causes them to seek optimal distinction through inclusion in some groups and differentiation from others. Earlier in this chapter we introduced the concept of networks of associations that we hold in our memory – called schemas. It is natural to us to build these schemas by assimilating like things and contrasting unlike things. We do it with cats and dogs, farms and shopping malls and with people. Some people are artistic, some are athletic, and some are neither of these things. Categorisation helps us learn and choose ways to respond to others. It is difficult to conceive how we might live very long if we could not categorise others. Categorisation provides us with a mental shortcut. It improves our ability to recall from our memory and saves cognitive resources, allowing us to perform better at the borders of processing capabilities, such as when we are performing multiple tasks. It assists us in fulfilling our need for meaning and coherence in life by providing a platform for shared comparisons. Shared beliefs can take on validity and appropriateness because others who are similar share similar beliefs.

Unfortunately, categorisation also has negative consequences. Group identity may become a convenient, even if incorrect, way to attribute success and failure, development and lack of development, moral and immoral cultural beliefs and many other shortcuts in the thinking and categorising process that people seem to use universally. As we form in-groups and out-groups in an attempt to achieve positive social identity, we overemphasise similarities and contrasts between in-groups and out-groups. This can have especially bad consequences in a country undergoing rapid social change. How does one effectively organise schemas when the boundaries between groups change rapidly? Which characteristics capture salience, exclusiveness or positive distinction? Current research is attempting to answer such questions.

Rapid automatic processes

While we don't entirely understand how the rapid pace of social change affects identity or the organisation of related schemas, we do know quite a bit about how the categorisation process works. Categorisation is a rapid and automatic process that occurs normally as part of cognition. Studies consistently show that in-group/out-group distinctions lead to very powerful stereotypes and incentives to conformity that have the potential to overrule our senses[24]. African-Americans have a higher probability of being convicted of violent crime than white Americans (not because of race but because of poverty and other social facts that can be traced to historic discrimination and unequal opportunity). Students in my class at Ohio State were exposed to years of TV news and other images that conditioned them to assume that our professor's attacker was an African-American. They perceived the person to be a man and to be physically more imposing because, given their experiences in life, they did not reasonably expect a woman of such size to shout obscenities in public, knock a professor to the ground or physically intimidate the well-built man who had started to rise from his chair to protect the professor.

By the way, what gender were the campus police officers who arrested the attacker in my university class?

The rapid and automatic nature of the categorisation process has been demonstrated in numerous studies. One popular type of study *primes* participants by rapidly exposing them to words designed to stimulate in-group/out-group distinctions (e.g. 'black', 'white', 'male', 'female', 'old', 'young', 'we' or 'they') and then following immediately with a request to perform a task. Typical tasks include calling out recognised words or classifying pictures or other stimuli. For example, researchers might ask respondents to indicate whether two strings of letters are both words, to call out a quickly shown stereotypical trait adjective (e.g. 'clean', 'ambitious', 'lazy', 'stupid') as soon as it's recognised (timing the response), or to sort photographs of people into groups containing similar people. People match primes to targets more quickly when the prime and target share stereotypical meaning. For instance, one would expect the words 'black rugby player' to be recognised more slowly than the words 'white rugby player' because of the few black rugby players in national sides, in South Africa or elsewhere. Gender, race and age lead to categorisation advantages in speed. Even when primes have been followed by trait adjectives as quickly as 55/1000 of a second, results have shown significant preconscious and postconscious in-group favouritism (e.g. an advantage such as faster response times for words associated with the in-group).

Categorisation and prejudice

One might reasonably conclude from the previous discussion that the process of categorising others is evidence of a deeply rooted human urge to be prejudiced against others – but that would be a very erroneous conclusion. Significantly, studies show similar results for stereotyping by high and low prejudiced people, causing influential researchers to conclude that automatic acquaintance with a negative stereotype does not necessarily indicate an endorsement of it.[25] Research also generally supports Marilynn Brewer's conclusion that in-group favouritism is not so much an act of out-group derogation so much as it is one of in-group favouritism.[26]

People characterise others, in part, to maintain the coherence and consistency of their own identity. Thus they will defend their identity against threats to personal and group self-esteem. They will pursue social mobility, social creativity or social conflict strategies in order to avoid stigmatisation and depreciation of identity. Change threatens social position, social status and other aspects of identity. This suggests a great question: by encouraging people to ignore racial identity, are people creating circumstances that may lead to even greater racial categorisation and racial group identity?[27]

Components of identity

In the previous sections of this chapter, we have focused on identity and its effects. In this section, we focus on the structure of identity. The structure of personal, relational and social identities can be traced to three types of differences: observable characteristics, personality traits and values. Although the first of these, which includes race and ethnicity, was artificially exaggerated under Apartheid rule, the latter two types of characteristics deserve equal or greater attention by those seriously interested in understanding South African identity differences.

Categorical attributes

A categorical attribute is some characteristic of a person that helps define their role, status and meaning in society. Ask someone on the street which categorical attributes define South African groups best and there is little doubt that most people would mention age, gender, ethnicity or race. These characteristics are among the easiest and perhaps most primitive categories into which people categorise others. People use innumerable categorical attributes to define the social groups to which individuals belong, in which they invest their energy and with which they identify themselves.[28] Parent-child, executive-worker, teacher-learner, elder-child, scuba diver-runner – even in a world in which hierarchy is less and less important, such words are charged with meaning and information about status relationships.

Influence of categorical attributes on South African behaviour

Many types of categorical attributes, such as those related to parental or occupational roles, require little explanation as regards influence on behaviour. Living standards are an attribute that may require further explanation. During the 1980s, marketers increasingly looked for ways to describe South African consumers that would avoid the use of Apartheid racial classification. Pioneering work overseas in other developing countries caught the attention of local marketers. Measures of living standards, such as the type of dwelling, electrification, water source, ownership of a radio, television, motor car, floor polisher or vacuum cleaner, or telephone, began to be included in the South African Advertising Research Foundation's *All Media and Product Survey* (AMPS). The AMPS and its progenitor, the great Wally Langschmidt, pioneered media and product consumption research. South Africa remains a world leader in the area.

Living standard measures influence behaviour directly. People who have growing incomes and no television are more likely to buy one. People who have electricity are more likely to use a range of labour-saving household appliances, if they can afford to buy them. Living standards, such as ownership of a certain brand of car, also influence behaviour indirectly by acting as markers of social class.

Personality traits

A personality trait is a relatively stable personality characteristic upon which people differ. Traits describe the characteristic ways in which people are likely to behave in most situations. Thousands of personality traits have been identified – Allport and Odbert identified 18,000 in the Webster's dictionary alone.[29] They include behavioural predispositions such as friendly, aggressive, masculine, anxious, calm or extroverted. During the last two decades, personality theorists have explored the structure of personality in an attempt to find a common structure underlying the incredible complexity of personality traits. Most of that work has concerned the so-called 'Big Five' factors of personality:[30] Openness to change, Conscientiousness, Extraversion, Agreeableness and Neuroticism (easily remembered by the mnemonic OCEAN). Factors are underlying dimensions that are identified using multivariate statistical techniques, such as exploratory factor analysis or multidimensional scaling.

Because the trait factors refer to underlying dimensions of personality, not types of people, all people can be thought of as possessing some amount of each personality trait, with most people somewhere between the extremes of having or not having the trait. The Big Five are thought to be relatively universal and have been observed in every region of the world. Research has shown that they are relatively stable during a person's life, from early adulthood to the retirement years. In part this is thought to be because of genetic influence, although trait acquisition can probably be more likely thought of as sociobiological (i.e. influenced by social and biological forces).

Optimum stimulation level (OSL) is a personality trait that is receiving much attention from consumer researchers.[31] People derive stimulation from the environment in many different ways. OSL refers to the level of stimulation in life that a person considers to be ideal. Although many different theoretical frameworks explain OSL, all share the basic notion that people prefer intermediate levels of stimulation – not too much, not too little – but vary in the level of stimulation in life they consider to be ideal. OSL is thought to be learned through social influences and to be influenced by physical characteristics, perhaps even genetics.[32] It rises in early adulthood and then declines with age. Men also appear to have higher OSL levels. People with high OSLs prefer environments characterised by stimulation, discontinuity, novelty, complexity, incongruity, change and ambiguity. Dogmatism, rigidity and intolerance of ambiguity are personality traits that correlate negatively with OSL.[33]

People with high OSLs have long been thought to be more innovative consumers who are more likely to purchase new products and new brands.[34] Although consumer behaviour models often assume that consumers engage in purposeful and goal-directed behaviour, consumers often seek thrills, adventure, disinhibition, new experiences, unfamiliarity and an alternative to familiar things for the express reason of raising their level of stimulation in life. This suggests that the goal, or intended reward, of these so-called *exploratory consumer behaviours* is intrinsic to the behaviour itself (i.e. the stimulation derived from the behaviour is the intended goal).

Influence of OSL on South African behaviour

Although little work on OSL has been reported in South Africa, work that has emerged from the SA Tribes project has been very supportive. Burgess and Harris[35] report that high and low OSL consumers differ as expected on gender, age, home language, employment status and level of formal education. Xhosa-speakers had the lowest overall OSL scores and Tsonga/Shangaan and Northern Sotho speakers the highest. People reporting Afrikaans or English as their home language scored slightly below the mean South African OSL score. OSL scores generally increased as formal education increased. They were unable to report any relation of interest between OSL and living standards, but they did report substantial differences in the product usage, brand loyalty and lifestyle interests of high and low OSL consumers.

Optimum stimulation scores for the traditional four race groups are reported for the 1997–1999 period in Chapter 3, along with the importance of personal values. The scores remain relatively stable over the period.

Clearly, OSL is of interest in any study that purports to understand the effect of change on consumers. Not only can we begin to understand how change or stability affect preferences for new products and services, we can also understand the relationship between personality, purchase and consumption preferences when consumers live in circumstances of rapid social and economic change.

Values

Just before the liberation of the Nazi death camp at Auschwitz, a small Jewish man sat in the depths of despair. The prisoner was the famous psychologist Victor Frankl. Prison guards had just found and destroyed the scraps of paper upon which he had been writing down a new theory of psychology. The incident drove Frankl to consider committing suicide by running for the prison fences but he soon realised that it illustrated, in a way not possible otherwise, the correctness of his theory.

Frankl's theory proposed that human behaviour is motivated by a 'will to meaning'.[36] Meaning, in turn, is derived from the attainment of one's values (core goals in life, see below). Frankl developed his theory while observing fellow inmates. Some inmates placed much importance on the value of *benevolence* (see Table 1 on p. 28). They spent their day checking on the welfare of fellow inmates, bolstering them and caring for their needs. Some placed high importance on *tradition*. They may have acted on this by saying prayers in a specific way or making their beds daily – as they had before captivity – even if the bed only had well-worn blankets and no linen. Frankl noticed that people who died often lost the meaning that they derived from these values prior to death. He reasoned that the achievement of values was core to the successful functioning of humans because value attainment was the source of meaning that people seek universally.

Frankl's desire to end his life because he had placed so much value on originating a new theory of psychology – the meaning of which he was temporarily unable to separate from the paper that had been destroyed – reinforced his belief in the power of meaning in one's life. It was days before Frankl could comfortably realise that destroying the paper could not destroy a theory that lived in his mind. The liberation of Auschwitz shortly after the incident allowed us to witness one of the great testimonies to the futility of racism. Frankl completed his theory and contributed to the psychological well-being of humankind well into the new millennium!

Social psychology literature is characterised by the notion that people have central and secondary dispositions that motivate their behaviour.[37] Central dispositions are not limited to a particular behavioural domain, such as consumer behaviour, but instead apply to a wide range of situations, contexts and behaviours. Personality traits, values and lifestyle feature prominently in many studies of social influence. Traits and values are central dispositions that are related but distinct concepts.[38] Traits are fixed central dispositions. They can be thought of as tendencies to behave in stable and predictable ways.

Values are enduring central dispositions, slow to change but not fixed.[39] According to the most widely accepted theory on human values, values refer to desirable, transsituational goals, varying in importance, that serve as guiding principles in people's lives.[40] *Lifestyle*, in comparison, is a secondary disposition that is especially important in the consumer context.[41] It is a summary measure that includes a person's activities, interests and opinions.

Attitudes are another secondary disposition. Attitudes are beliefs about affect (liking), behaviour (doing) and cognition (knowing) that are linked to specific situations.

Secondary dispositions, such as lifestyle and attitudes, are affected by central dispositions. Furthermore, central and secondary dispositions affect behaviour. For instance, consider a person who buys a particular brand (behaviour) or votes for a political party (behaviour). The person may have many reasons but let's consider one: he believes the manufacturer or political party supports a clean environment (attitude). If we observe this person's life, we may well find that he recycles glass products (lifestyle), attends Greenpeace meetings (lifestyle) and participates in an environmental chat room on the Internet (lifestyle). If we should measure his values and traits, we will probably find that he places much importance on universalism (concern for greater humanity, animals and the environment) and that he scores high on conscientiousness and caring. Furthermore, we can expect statistically significant relations between all of these characteristics.

The Schwartz Theory on the Content and Structure of Human Values

Prior to the work of social psychologist Milton Rokeach in the 1970s,[42] the values concept suffered from the lack of a precise and widely accepted definition.[43] Another social psychologist, Shalom Schwartz, has extended Rokeach's work by refining the values concept. Schwartz has originated a theory of the content and structure of human values. He has devised instruments to test the theory and produced supportive results from studies conducted in more than 60 countries in every inhabited region of the world, including South Africa.[44] Schwartz defines values as desirable, transsituational goals, that vary in importance and serve as guiding principles in people's lives. His theory identifies a comprehensive set of ten motivationally distinct values that constitute the content of human values. These value types are derived from Schwartz's analysis of the universal requirements with which all individuals and societies must cope as biological, psychological and social beings. The relative importance of a particular value type will reflect its contribution to the psychological and social functioning of the individual; that is, its contribution to the attainment of goals crucial for preserving societies, relationships and individual well-being.[45] Table 1 provides definitions of each motivational value type in terms of its central goal and lists exemplary specific values that primarily express the goal of the type.

Schwartz's theory proposes well-defined and dynamic structural relations among the ten types of values (i.e. the structure of human values).[46] The

Table 1: *Motivational value types, definitions and exemplary values (Schwartz, 1992)*

Value type	Definition	Exemplary values
Power	Social status and prestige, control or dominance over people and resources	Social power, authority, wealth
Achievement	Personal success through demonstrating competence according to social standards	Success, ability, ambition
Hedonism	Pleasure and sensuous gratification for oneself	Pleasure, fun, fulfilment
Stimulation	Excitement, novelty and challenge in life	Excitement, variety
Self-direction	Independent of thought and action, creating, exploring	Creativity, curiosity, freedom
Universalism	Understanding, appreciation, tolerance, and protection for the welfare of all people and nature	Social justice, equality, awareness
Benevolence	Preservation and enhancement of the welfare of people with whom one is in frequent personal contact	Kindness, support, honesty, forgiveness
Tradition	Respect, commitment towards and acceptance of the customs and ideas that culture or religion provide	Deference, devotion, tolerance
Conformity	Restraint of actions, inclinations and impulses likely to upset or harm others and violate social expectations or norms	Courtesy, obedience, honour
Security	Safety, harmony and stability of society, of relationships and of self	Social order, organisation

pursuit of any value has consequences that may conflict or may be congruent with the pursuit of other values. For example, the time demands required to pursue ambition or success (achievement values) may conflict with one's desire to maintain close extended family relations (benevolence values). However, the very same pursuit of career success will be compatible with the pursuit of control over others (power values) as both motivate dominance over the environment for personal gain.

The pattern of compatibilities and conflicts in the theory gives rise to a motivational continuum, which can be represented by a circular arrangement of the values (see Figure 1). The closer any two values in either direction around the circle, the more similar their underlying motivations. The more distant any two values, the more antagonistic their underlying motivations. This structure is a *circumplex*, except for tradition outside conformity. The theory holds that the ten value types can be summarised by two higher order *value domains*. *Self-enhancement vs self-transcendence* opposes power and achievement against universalism and benevolence. Both of the former

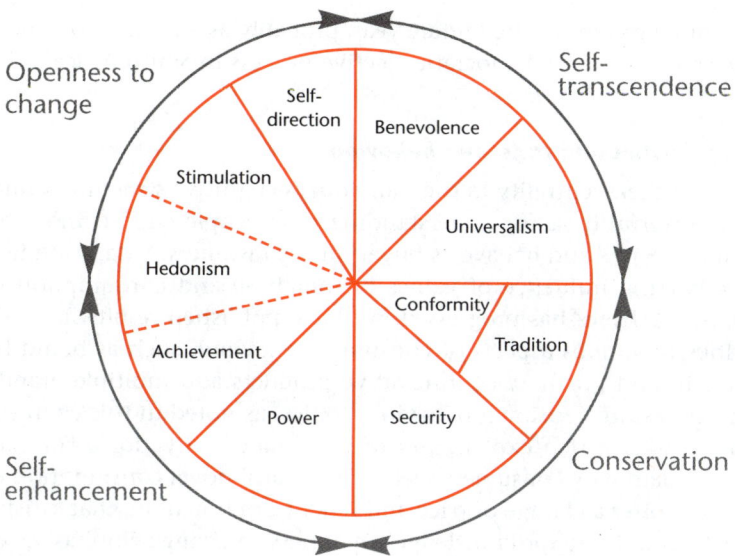

Figure 1: *Motivational value types and higher order value domains (Schwartz, 1992)*

emphasise pursuit of self-interests, whereas the latter pair involve concern for the welfare and interests of others. *Openness to change vs conservation* opposes self-direction and stimulation against security, conformity and tradition. The former emphasises independent action, thought, and feeling and readiness for new experience, whereas the latter emphasise self-restriction, order and resistance to change. Hedonism values share elements of both openness and self-enhancement.

The next chapter includes a series of tables reporting South African value priorities in 1997, 1998, 1999 and 2001 as measured by SA Tribes and for which we have provided extensive information concerning the reliability and validity across the four populations.[47] The table is remarkable for a number of reasons. First, it is clear that race is of very little importance if one wishes to understand differences in the value priorities of South Africans. Security, benevolence and universalism are the most important; stimulation, hedonism and achievement are the least important values to all four populations. Second, and most remarkable, is the incredible stability. The mean ratings of every value type (which were measured on a 6-point scale) move only hundredths of a point over the three years. There is one exception: the rating of power declines (by approximately one full point on the 6-point scale) for all groups in the middle year, probably as a result of a wider belief in the stability of the democratic elective process in South Africa.

Value priorities and consumer behaviour

Because of their centrality to the individual's cognitive structure, values provide a powerful basis for understanding how people choose and use products and services and behave as buyers and consumers.[48] Many studies have argued for the influence of values on purchase and consumption behaviours. As SA Tribes has progressed, we have published results linking value priorities to various aspects of consumer behaviour, such as brand loyalty, interest in and purchase of innovative products and multiple brands, and other interesting consumer behaviour topics, as noted in this chapter.

Values offer a rich explanation of consumer motivations. For example, values explain why consumers seek exciting and novel consumption experiences that offer a change of pace and relief from boredom; that satisfy one's curiosity and desire for knowledge. Openness to change emphasises exploration and favours novelty, variety and stimulation through change from established patterns. Thus, one may expect that the importance attached to this value domain will have a positive effect on the number of brands used and consumption of innovative products. Conservation emphasises submissive self-restriction, preservation of traditional practices and the protection of stability. The importance given to conservation values should have a negative effect on these two types of behaviour.[49] The value domains of self-enhancement and self-transcendence appear less relevant for predicting brand switching and consumption of innovative products. They deal with the pursuit of one's own relative success and dominance over others, versus emphasising acceptance of others as equals and concern for their welfare. Thus, one may hypothesise that these value domains will be less important for explaining brand switching and consumption of innovative products. We can also make similar hypotheses about how consumers perceive advertising. For instance, consider the Nordic Ice advertisement we tested in South Africa and the United States (see Figure 2).[50]

The results of the study were noteworthy. Almost identical proportions of students at Wits University and at Ohio State University[51] perceived the model to have values related to stimulation, hedonism and self-direction, suggesting the incredible stability of values perceptions across cultures. Moreover, the results indicated that the model's image was sufficient to trigger the influence of values on consumer reactions to the advertisement – indicating that the choice of models in ads is far more than finding a

Figure 2: *Nordic Ice advertisement*

pretty face, whether in the USA or South Africa. The physical attractiveness and similarity to the audience of a model's image portrayed in an advertisement trigger deeply held values that in turn affect a consumer's response to the advertisement. Such results indicate not only the importance of understanding the effect of value priorities but also the mechanisms by which such effects are triggered.

Identity, values and culture

Much is made of cultural differences between various ethnic groups in South Africa. Culture and values are related concepts, so it is natural that a moment is taken to discuss cultural differences and identity. Culture and values are often equated in error. Culture includes far more than the concept of values. Instead, it refers to a cohesive set of values, attitudes and beliefs that emerge in adaptation to the environment.

Because values underlie attitudes and even more situationally bound beliefs as part of the belief system, culture has the potential to lead to normative behaviour and to invest behaviour with meaning. People are often very unaware of the influence of culture. This is because it is effortlessly internalised from birth. As we learn values, beliefs, attitudes and behaviours from our parents and other influential people, we are taking in their culture and learning about normative behaviours.

Cialdini and his associates have systematically investigated normative influence.[52] They suggest that norms are activated by situational cues. Rapid change – as is experienced by many South Africans as a result of urbanisation, greater access to globalised media, or changes in any other social, economic or political factors – may impact on the stability of adherence to cultural norms because it results in important changes to the situational cues that instigate normative influence.

This is clear when one considers the major types of normative influence that impact on the individual. *Injunctive norms* refer to behaviours thought to be socially acceptable or approved by others. *Subjective norms* refer to behaviours that are encouraged or discouraged by people who are important to me. *Personal norms* flow from internalised values with the objective of enhancing or preserving one's sense of self-worth and avoiding self-concept distress.[53] In situations marked by rapid change, the cues that trigger normative influence may change dramatically. Injunctive and subjective norms may become less clear or have little relevance because of the changing circumstances. Furthermore, personal norms may clash with subjective or injunctive norms.

The increasing complexity of cultural influence is perhaps most easily conceived if one imagines an individual coping with life situations that are characterised by unfamiliar circumstances. When injunctive and subjective norms fail to have relevance, people are forced to create personal norms, which in turn become cultural norms if adopted by enough people. When norms are in a state of flux, as must be the case in many South African homes, organisations that hope to influence people and serve their needs must be sensitive to the changing normative landscape.

Individualism and collectivism

Understanding the changing normative landscape may be aided by understanding the forces of individualism and collectivism. Researchers have invested considerable effort in understanding how behaviour shapes and maintains social order. The interplay of individualism and collectivism has received much of this attention.[54] Collectivism has been defined as a generalised sense of concern for others. In suggesting that a person becomes a person through other people, the African philosophy of *ubuntu* encourages a collectivist orientation toward life that is evident in the value orientations of South Africans of all races. It is noted in the high relative importance of self-transcendence and conservation values.

Collectivism is thought to be a by-product of agrarian cultures, in which the unit of survival is food and families are large[55]. In fact, many characteristics associated with most and least developed sectors of the South African population may act as antecedents ('causes') of individualism or collectivism.[56] All societies have mixtures of collectivism and individualism. Where collectivism is high, societies are more likely to have strong family structures that place much importance on family integrity. People are more likely to define themselves in terms of their in-group, which they see as relatively homogeneous and strongly differentiated from out-groups. The in-group is seen to have a defined hierarchy that has a legitimate role to play in regulating the behaviour of its members in order to maintain harmony, which may include subordinating personal goals to achieve group goals and personal compromises that allow face-saving by others in the group. Behaviour is intimate, requiring one to give social support and to play social roles that reflect interdependence and duty.

Migration, cultural complexity, urbanism and affluence are powerful forces that shift social orientations toward individualism.[57] Individualism encourages the primacy of individual goals and the necessary social behaviour to accomplish them, even if that requires confrontation with others. People feel an emotional detachment from others and weigh up the costs and benefits of their behaviour in terms of their own attitudes and beliefs. Individualism results in societies where socialisation takes place in order to accomplish self-reliance and independence, discouraging obedience and duty to groups that are not perceived to have legitimacy to direct personal behaviour in any event.

Although results of research on individualism and collectivism generally have confirmed these expectations, it seems reasonable to be cautious about trying to apply these findings in an emerging economy and transitional society such as South Africa until such time as we have more conclusive evidence about the applicability of these concepts. Schwartz, for instance, has challenged the individualism-collectivism concept,[58] noting that his extensive values data suggests that values can serve individual, collective and mixed interests. Sussman has also noted the paucity of knowledge about cultural transitions.[59]

Conclusion

This chapter has provided a brief overview of identity, its structure and its influences on human behaviour. Identity is a summary construct that encompasses 'who we are, how we live and what we want from life'. It seems to be intrinsic to the human categorisation processes, to be automatic in its influence and rich in its meaning. Although it is not fixed, it is enduring and slow to change. The structure of identity is comprised of values, traits and categorical attributes – three classes of human characteristics that researchers have spent considerable effort investigating and linking to human behaviour. However, although we understand some influences of these characteristics very well, we know less about the stability of identity or its influence on behaviour in emerging economies and transitional societies. The next chapter introduces an organising framework for understanding identity influence in South Africa and then introduces the 16 tribes.

3: Introducing the tribes
Who they are and how they were identified

As the previous chapter suggests, identity is a complex web of interrelated concepts that people hold about who they are, how they live and what they want from life. Some of these concepts refer to characteristics that are easily observable by others (gender, height, type of residence). Others refer to roles that people take on in certain situations (teacher, parent, patient, wife). Still other concepts refer to beliefs, attitudes or values that may be visible or invisible (environmentalist, egalitarianist). Identity concepts share one commonality across their great diversity: they refer to aspects of human existence to which people attribute such importance that they internalise and draw meaning from them.

Identity is at the crux of the great debate about the role of race in describing South Africans and their behaviour. The legacy of South Africa's 20th century social engineering experiment is demonstrated daily in the great discrepancies of access to resources – wealth, health and knowledge – that continue to affect most people of differing Apartheid racial groups. But how meaningful are these racial groups now that a new government has been in place for some time? Are they now or were they ever really groups? What is the real fruit of the policies of the past and what does that imply for the future?

As we embarked on the SA Tribes research programme, it was common cause that identity would be affected by the dramatic social, political and economic changes that were taking place in South African society. Affirmative action programmes would increase access to schools, universities and other institutions where knowledge and values are acquired. Increasing access to safe drinking water, electricity, housing and health care would have the effect of uplifting other aspects of human development. The hierarchical nature of racial relations, removed already by law, would begin to disappear in private life. The new government was prepared to address issues of equality as regards not only race but also gender, physical capability and sexual orientation. White South Africans would no longer be the pariahs of the world and would have their first real opportunity to fully contemplate their identity as Africans and their role on the continent with their fellow Africans.

All of this was very interesting in its own right, but I was quite preoccupied with the thought that the changes in South Africa – unique as they may be – mirrored changes in other transitional societies and emerging economies. Anyone who has attended one of my talks or courses knows my passion for this topic and the Indian Ocean Rim, so I will not dwell on it here except to say that I am surprised how few people seem to realise that nearly six out of ten people in the world reside in the 25 emerging economies *The Economist* magazine reports on in each issue.[1] These countries represent the majority of humankind. Their economies are growing faster than the most developed countries. Many are beginning to emerge as consumer nations in every possible way. China now accounts for more unit sales in products such as refrigerators, microwaves and other categories than the United States.[2] South Africans are waking up to the reality that these countries are not simply becoming important, they are important.

In the early 1980s, many speakers used to tell executive audiences that there was 'no such thing as a Black market, the Black market is THE market'. In the same sense, there is no such thing as an emerging market in the longer term of world market development. During the next 25 years, emerging economy consumers will increasingly dictate the pace of innovation and product development across the entire spectrum of products and services. Think about that a moment. How will global media be influenced when people in Muslim nations, such as Indonesia or Malaysia, begin to really influence product content? What would happen when African markets began to develop to the extent that they could wield real economic power?

Thoughts such as these caused me to consider more deeply the changing social identities of my adopted homeland. After a brief visit to Israel – during which I was fortunate to visit with Shalom Schwartz and learn about the development of a new values scale that is designed to measure values in countries such as South Africa – I called another old friend, Sue Grant, who was then Managing Director of Markinor. Sue was immediately supportive of the idea of a study that might produce more reliable information about value priorities in South Africa. I had begun collaborating by that time on research of personality traits with Jan-Benedict E. M. Steenkamp and so a study of identity began to take shape. Sue called in Markinor director Mari Harris, one of the top socio-political researchers in South Africa, and, with her strong support, we set out on the journey that has resulted in this book. I acknowledge, where used, additional research data provided by corporate sponsors and, in some cases, the assistance of graduate students under my supervision. The SA Tribes project would not have been possible without the contributions of all of these people.

This chapter briefly reports on the research methodology that we followed for the three main national surveys that form the backbone of the programme. It then briefly introduces the four major groupings of tribes that emerge from the analysis.

The research methodology is important because it explains how we identified the tribes. It will be evident immediately that we have taken precautions to enhance the reliability and validity of our data across cultures. These precautions include aspects of the research design, survey design, interview procedure and analysis. Our goal was to increase the confidence in our findings by providing readers with the information they require to judge our performance. However, we realise that most people who read this book do not have extensive interest in detailed statistical analyses or methodological debate. So, if you are a professional researcher, you will find ample directions to more academic publications where we report cross-national measurement invariance and other more technical information about the reliability and validity of our data.

The introduction of the four major groupings introduces the general structure of the SA Tribes project. It is very helpful in understanding the more detailed information presented in the four chapters that follow.

Identifying the tribes

This section concerns the research methodology we pursued in the three main waves of in-home interviews that constitute the major data source of the SA Tribes research programme. We begin by briefly sketching a model of identity influence (Fig. 3), which helps explain why we chose the variables used in the study.

The discussion in the previous chapter indicated the interrelations of situation, identity and behaviour. The movement from situation to situation is characteristic of life. We leave home, visit the shopping mall, watch a football match, have dinner with friends. As each situation changes, various aspects of our identity are activated. Consider the ability of two dinners at the same table in the same restaurant to evoke very different identity elements. The first dinner is a family gathering celebrating a family member's accomplishment, perhaps a child's matriculation. The second is a business dinner with the management team from a prospective client. Which categorical attributes, values and personality traits will each situation activate? What accounts for the differences? The answer is that a situation includes not only its physical elements but also its social and temporal elements (i.e. people and time). If the celebratory dinner with the same family members

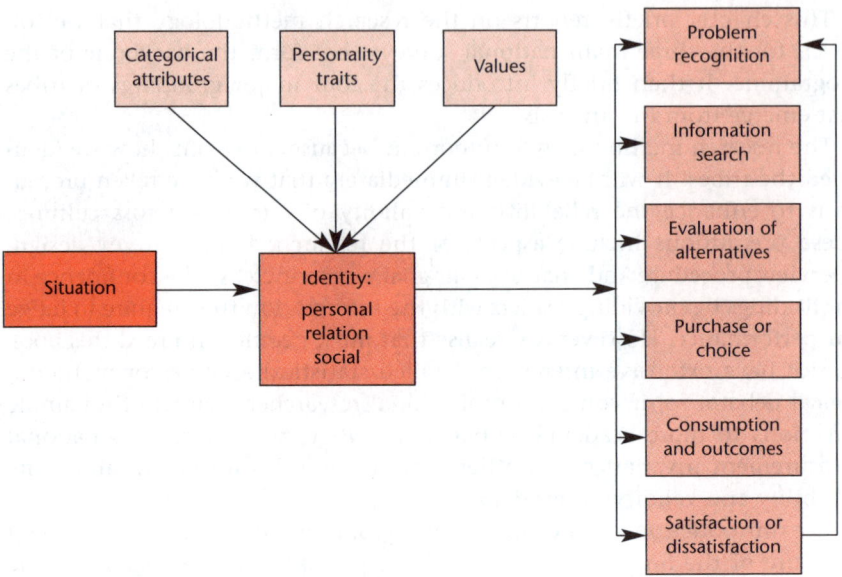

Figure 3: *SA Tribes model of identity influence*

took place a month later, it might be very different. People bring the emotional baggage from the day with them to each situation. They can attend to and process various aspects of the situations in which they find themselves differently; different people may process them in different ways. Nevertheless in most cases they will process them in the same way.

The situation may activate the influence of personal, relational or social identities, individually or in combinations. Our model holds that all of these types of identity will influence the problems people recognise, the way they search for information and evaluate alternative solutions, the actions they take; even their evaluations of satisfaction that emerge.

The apparent simplicity of this model obscures an incredible complexity that exists in a society characterised by wide variations in human development, such as South Africa. How similar are the problems that are likely to be recognised in the span of an average day by a Sandton executive and the Alexandra informal settlement dweller just a few kilometres away? Very different problems emerge. Now compare that Alexandra resident to someone in the rural areas surrounding East London. Again, very different problems emerge when the two are compared. Our awareness of these differences guided our selection of the characteristics we measured in the household surveys, as well as the design of our sampling strategy.

Characteristics used to form identity groups

Assumptions must be made in any segmentation scheme. The South African Advertising Research Foundation (SAARF) living standard measure (LSM) scheme assumes that a subset of the living standard measures we measure in SA Tribes will reasonably predict media and product consumption. Many service providers find it useful to segment people into groups based on even more simple measures, such as gender or ability to pay. There is not really any right or wrong way to segment people into groups, so long as the result works, proper statistical techniques are used and the methodology can be justified by the theory that motivated the segmentation exercise.

The SA Tribes methodology makes the assumption that the 'tribes' generally behave in a similar way. This is because of the enduring nature of the values, personality traits and many of the categorical attributes that define an individual's identity and also because of the relative stability of the situational factors people encounter in daily life. For example, the Sandton executive mentioned earlier is very unlikely to encounter the living standard constraints that define many of the situational forces acting on the Alexandra informal settlement resident, even though they are practically in sight of one another much of the day. This is an unpleasant legacy of the past. We feel that our assumptions are reasonable and, in fact, much less restricting than any other scheme of which we are aware.

In SA Tribes, people are segmented based on their propensity to experience certain situations and on their identity characteristics (i.e. categorical attributes, values and personality traits). These relations are depicted in Figure 3. Categorical attributes measured included demographic characteristics, measures of participation in the formal financial sector and measures of living standards. In most cases, the shared set of living standards variables were operationalised (written in the questionnaire) exactly as they appear in AMPS research and in all cases the order of the individual questions in the major scales was rotated so that every questionnaire was different and no pattern of response emerged simply as a result of the order in which we presented the questions.

Demographic characteristics included age of respondent, age of all people in the household, education, gender, home language, marital status, race, religious denomination, religiosity, frequency of religious practice, total monthly household income.

Measures of participation in the formal financial sector included grocery outlets frequented, responsibility for daily household purchases, type of bank account (cheque or current account, savings account, transmission account, investment/subscription/paid-up shares, credit card, petrol or garage card, ATM card, loan, none of these), types of assurance and insurance policies (whole life, endowments, savings, investment policy, retirement annuity, personal pension policy, funeral, medical, short-term, other, none of these) and working status.

Living standard measures included access to the Internet on a personal computer at home, access to a cellular telephone, access to a personal computer at home, dishwashing liquid, domestic servant or helper, DStv, durable items bought on credit in last few months, dwelling type, electricity, electricity switch on, floor polisher or vacuum cleaner, flush toilets in or outside house, fridge or freezer, hi-fi or music centre, hot running water from a geyser, microwave oven, M-Net, motor car, running water, television set, washing machine, water laid on, telephone in the home, telephone working, telephone directory, or having none of these things. A list of 40 lifestyle interests was also measured.

The personality trait of most interest to us in the SA Tribes project is optimum stimulation level (OSL). Steenkamp and Baumgartner concluded that Garlington and Shimota's 95-item Change Seeker Index (CSI) is a preferred instrument to measure OSL.[3] However, a 95-item survey was inappropriate for the current research. This is not only because such length would excessively tire respondents, but also because longer surveys present more difficulty to people who have been deprived of a formal education. Reducing the cognitive demands of the survey obviously improves the chances for a more reliable and valid measure across a diverse population such as South Africa. Researchers accomplish this by using shortened scales. In SA Tribes, OSL was measured using a shortened scale developed by Steenkamp and Baumgartner in Europe and validated cross-culturally in Belgium, the Netherlands, Great Britain and the USA.[4] The scale consists of only seven items but their findings indicated that, compared to the original scale, the shortened scale not only reduced the data collection burden for the respondent but has also improved nomological validity and psychometric properties. CSI is typically rated on a 5-point Likert scale. However, in the present study, we use the same 6-point scale as used for the measurement of value priorities (see next page) to reduce potential respondent confusion. Before analyses, scores were reversed so that high ratings indicate high OSL. As we have reported elsewhere, the scale performed exceptionally well in the current research, exhibiting a high degree of measurement invariance across cultures.[5]

Values

We also achieved excellent reliability and validity using a shortened values scale developed recently by Schwartz, Lehmann and Roccas, called the *Portrait Values Questionnaire* (PVQ).[6] As noted in the previous chapter, Schwartz has proposed a theory of the content and structure of human values, developed instruments to test it and provided supportive results from more than 65 countries on every inhabited continent. His theory of value content and structure may be the most validated in the history of psychology. The standard 57-item *Schwartz Value Survey* (SVS) has been used extensively to test the theory.

In a few instances,[7] including a small test of university students conducted at Potchefstroom University, the proposed content and structure failed to emerge. Very young and very old respondents also sometimes produced similar results. Schwartz concluded that his values scale, rather than the theory, might be the cause. He reasoned that the standard 57-item scale might not be suitable because of its length and high level of abstraction and he set out to develop a shortened version of the scale.[8] The availability of the new shortened values scale permits values research to be extended to many ECMs not studied effectively in the past.[9]

The PVQ includes short, textual portraits of 29 different people. Each portrait describes a person to whom certain goals, aspirations and wishes – all expressive of the same single value type – are important. For each portrait, respondents answer: 'How much like you is this person?' They check one of six boxes labelled: 'very much like me', 'like me', 'somewhat like me', 'a little like me', 'not like me' and 'not like me at all'. In our research we added a seventh box labelled 'do not know' in order to lessen the incidence of 'I-can-answer-any-question' bias and courtesy bias,[10] and to encourage respondents who found a particular scale item too challenging to respond accurately. Before analysis, scores were reversed so that high ratings indicated high value importance and 'don't know' respondents were dropped.

Schwartz has presented evidence that the PVQ and the SVS measure the same motivational value types.[11] However, the PVQ takes much less time to complete (usually less than 10 minutes versus on average 25 minutes for the SVS), and is cognitively less demanding. An index of the importance of a value type was obtained by averaging the ratings for the values within the value type in question. Similarly, the importance of a value domain was obtained by averaging the importances attributed to the value types within each domain. Schwartz argues that hedonism is related both to openness to change and to self-enhancement. Hence, we excluded hedonism from the computation of the importance attached to value domains. This procedure ensures equal weighting of all values (value types) in the construction of a particular value type (value domain).[12]

The reliability and validity of the analyses were tested using the configural verification approach detailed in Schwartz.[13] This approach entails using similarity structure analysis, a multidimensional scaling technique, to examine the variable interrelations for the hypothesised structure. As we have reported elsewhere,[14] the PVQ provided highly reliable and valid data.

How we determined who to interview

Our analysis was conducted on data collected during in-home personal interviews by Markinor (Pty) Ltd, one of South Africa's largest and only ISO9000-certified market research firm. Markinor is internationally affiliated to Walker Research and Gallup; the Markinor Chairman sits on the Gallup International Board. Sampling was designed and conducted by Markinor to produce a nationally representative sample.

Personal interviews were conducted as part of a syndicated study of 3,500 South African households with residents over the age of 16. Marketers are

Table 2: *Value priorities and Optimum Stimulation Level 1997–1999*

Mean ratings	1997				1998			
	White	Black	Coloured	Asian	White	Black	Coloured	Asian
Benevolence	5.40	4.95	5.15	5.24	5.44	4.75	5.28	5.35
Universalism	5.01	4.93	5.00	5.06	5.01	4.76	5.14	5.13
Conformity	4.55	4.80	4.43	4.26	4.88	4.96	5.05	4.93
Tradition	4.47	4.57	4.42	4.57	4.34	4.47	4.50	4.68
Security	5.44	5.17	5.16	5.32	5.36	5.04	5.36	5.42
Power	4.07	4.57	3.98	4.34	3.08	3.71	2.85	2.84
Achievement	4.19	4.60	3.83	4.24	4.30	4.50	4.10	4.06
Hedonism	4.02	4.47	3.85	4.14	4.12	4.34	3.96	3.95
Stimulation	3.90	3.89	3.55	3.83	3.94	3.92	3.65	3.62
Self-direction	4.82	4.72	4.46	4.68	4.78	4.49	4.46	4.41
Self-transcendence	5.28	5.02	5.10	5.21	5.22	4.76	5.21	5.24
Conservation	4.51	4.69	4.43	4.41	4.86	4.82	4.97	5.01
Self-enhancement	4.13	4.59	3.90	4.17	3.69	4.11	3.47	3.45
Openness to change	4.36	4.30	4.01	4.26	4.39	4.22	4.10	4.08
Optimum Stimulation Level	18.37	19.47	17.28	18.03	18.81	19.38	17.58	17.85

Note: Values rated on 6-point scale and OSL scored on 30-point maximum scale.
Sample consists of valid responses from 3,500 interviews per year.

well acquainted with the All Media and Products Survey (AMPS), which is a demographic, media, and product consumption survey of over 17,000 homes conducted annually by the South African Advertising Research Foundation. It is the most authoritative source of media and consumption behaviour in South Africa and one of the most advanced surveys of its type in the world. Using AMPS and Markinor's extensive area database, a national area probability sample was drawn for traditional black residential areas (where mobility, urbanisation and informal housing creation result in significant population shifts) and a race, community and region stratified sample was drawn for all other areas. Age, gender, and working status controls were randomly assigned to sampling points in order to ensure representativeness. Neighbourhood racial composition continues to change in South Africa. When a respondent did not match the expected race assigned to a sampling point, the interview was conducted anyway; the research company database was updated and new sampling points were drawn in order to reach the overall racial sampling quota.

Extensive quality controls were implemented during the interviews. Three calls were made to each sampling point. The full range of dwelling types – including squatter camps – were included in the survey in metropolitan, urban, peri-urban, rural and deep-rural areas in all nine provinces.

1999			
White	Black	Coloured	Asian
5.45	4.84	5.20	4.97
4.99	4.82	5.04	5.11
4.88	5.00	5.00	4.87
4.38	4.59	4.51	4.57
5.28	5.05	5.22	5.24
3.12	3.90	2.73	2.87
4.16	4.55	4.07	4.09
4.19	4.45	4.08	3.86
3.97	4.06	3.77	3.71
4.88	4.61	4.60	4.44
5.22	4.83	5.12	5.21
4.85	4.88	4.91	4.90
3.64	4.22	3.40	4.05
4.43	4.34	4.19	4.08
18.86	20.17	17.14	17.78

Table 3: *Value priorities 1997–1999 in order of importance*

Ranked means	1997				1998			
	White	Black	Coloured	Asian	White	Black	Coloured	Asian
Security	5.44	5.17	5.16	5.32	5.36	5.04	5.36	5.4
Benevolence	5.40	4.95	5.15	5.24	5.44	4.75	5.28	5.3
Universalism	5.01	4.93	5.00	5.06	5.01	4.76	5.14	5.1
Conformity	4.55	4.80	4.43	4.26	4.88	4.96	5.05	4.9
Self-direction	4.82	4.72	4.46	4.68	4.78	4.49	4.46	4.4
Achievement	4.19	4.60	3.83	4.24	4.30	4.50	4.10	4.0
Tradition	4.47	4.57	4.42	4.57	4.34	4.47	4.50	4.6
Power	4.07	4.57	3.98	4.34	3.08	3.71	2.85	2.8
Hedonism	4.02	4.47	3.85	4.14	4.12	4.34	3.96	3.9
Stimulation	3.90	3.89	3.55	3.83	3.94	3.92	3.65	3.6
Self-transcendence	5.28	5.02	5.10	5.21	5.22	4.76	5.21	5.2
Conservation	4.51	4.69	4.43	4.41	4.86	4.82	4.97	5.0
Self-enhancement	4.13	4.59	3.90	4.17	3.69	4.11	3.47	3.4
Openness to change	4.36	4.30	4.01	4.26	4.39	4.22	4.10	4.0

Note: Sample is representative of magazine buyers in South Africa during November 2001, n=451.

Table 4: *The incredible stability of human values – Value priorities 2001 compared to 199...*

Mean ratings	2001				2001 compared to 1997			
	White	Black	Coloured	Asian	White	Black	Coloured	Asian
Benevolence	5.21	4.91	5.04	4.51	-0.19	-0.04	-0.11	-0.7
Universalism	5.44	4.97	5.41	5.07	0.43	0.04	0.41	0.0
Conformity	4.21	4.53	4.47	4.35	-0.34	-0.27	0.04	0.0
Tradition	4.30	4.53	4.87	4.53	-0.17	-0.04	0.45	-0.0
Security	5.34	5.16	5.34	5.00	-0.10	-0.01	0.18	-0.3
Power	3.41	3.59	2.34	3.49	-0.66	-0.98	-1.64	-0.8
Achievement	4.10	4.78	4.12	4.31	-0.09	0.18	0.29	0.0
Hedonism	4.39	4.65	3.71	4.53	0.37	0.18	-0.14	0.3
Stimulation	4.14	4.58	3.75	4.21	0.24	0.69	0.20	0.3
Self-direction	4.91	4.96	4.91	4.67	0.09	0.24	0.45	-0.0
Self-transcendence	5.21	4.94	5.22	4.79	-0.07	-0.08	0.12	-0.4
Conservation	4.61	4.74	4.89	4.63	0.10	0.05	0.46	0.2
Self-enhancement	3.75	4.19	3.23	3.90	-0.38	-0.40	-0.67	-0.2
Openness to change	4.52	4.77	4.33	4.44	0.16	0.47	0.32	0.1

1999			
White	Black	Coloured	Asian
5.28	5.05	5.22	5.24
5.45	4.84	5.20	4.97
4.99	4.82	5.04	5.11
4.88	5.00	5.00	4.87
4.88	4.61	4.60	4.44
4.16	4.55	4.07	4.09
4.38	4.59	4.51	4.57
3.12	3.90	2.73	2.87
4.19	4.45	4.08	3.86
3.97	4.06	3.77	3.71
5.22	4.83	5.12	5.21
4.85	4.88	4.91	4.90
3.64	4.22	3.40	4.05
4.43	4.34	4.19	4.08

After three calls to a dwelling the nearest dwelling was substituted. There was a minimum callback of 20% to verify sampling accuracy and interviewer compliance. Items were rotated in the questionnaire to remove the chance of order effects.

The surveys were conducted in the respondent's home language by professional interviewers, who were also trained to be sensitive to issues of social class, education, response bias and other issues that impact on the reliability and validity of results.

Removing respondents for response bias

It is vitally important for researchers to perform checks on the reliability and validity of the data they collect. The preceding discussion has made it clear that much of the work concerning reliability and validity occurs during the design of the questionnaire and planning of the fieldwork. It may not be obvious that we went to much trouble to identity short versions of the scales used in the survey in order to improve reliability and validity. Researchers are keenly aware that the more questions one asks in emerging economies, the greater the threat to reliability and validity.

Research is one of those things where less can be more. Here's one reason why. Pretend for a moment that you have agreed to be surveyed by the

Markinor interviewer. However, as the survey continues you realise that you do not really want to proceed. Yet, you have agreed. What do you do? Many people just provide any answer in order to move through the interview as quickly as possible. Other people may find the questions concern things they have never thought about before, or require answers that they don't care to provide.

If such people are included in the dataset that is analysed, they will then obscure real trends in the data. If they agree with everything, then the mean (average) score and the dispersion of scores around the mean will be inflated. If they just respond randomly, choosing high or low answers, the dispersion of responses and the mean may be affected as well. The result can be compared to listening to a radio station slightly off channel. The true tune will be obscured.

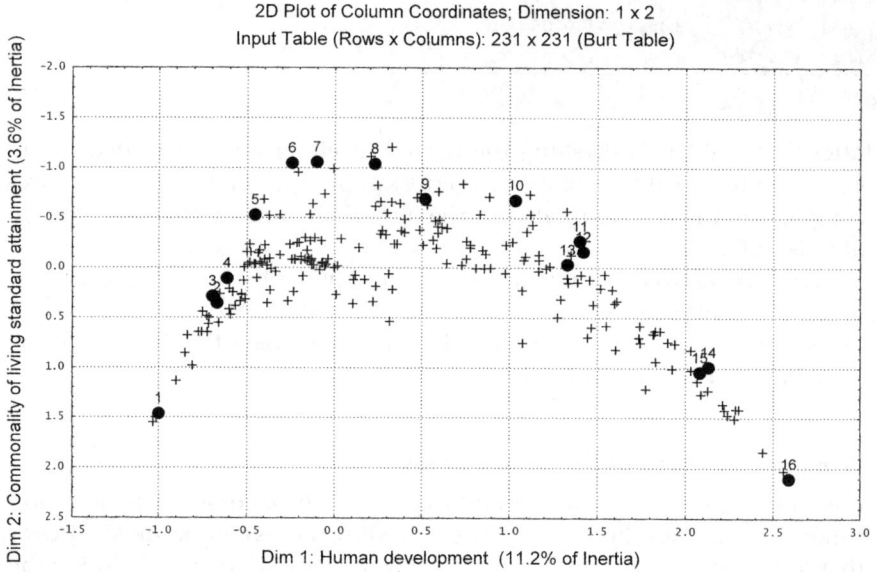

Figure 4: *Multiple correspondence analysis*

As we have reported in our more academic work, we dropped some respondents from the analysis. These included those who failed to respond or responded 'don't know' to a stimulus item on either the PVQ or CSI scale (about 9%); those who provided the same response for every item in the

7-item CSI scale including the negatively scored items (about 1%), or those who consecutively provided the same response for 15 or more items on the PVQ scale (less than .05%). This resulted in a total of about 10% of the respondents being dropped. When compared to the overall sample, the dropped respondents were somewhat more likely to be black (about 70% of the dropped respondents were black while 60% of the total sample were black) and to have not completed high school (a similar proportion). When we compared the association between being dropped with race or education the statistical tests indicated that there was very little cause for concern (Cramer's V < .085 on a scale of 0 to 1). The remaining respondents were then weighted to the AMPS population.

Four major groupings of the tribes

The identity characteristics of the respondents were analysed using cluster analysis in a two-step procedure.[15] Cluster analysis is a technique that identifies groups of respondents with similar responses to the identity characteristic questions that were included in the analysis from the survey. The technique allows one to choose among alternative numbers of clusters to find a solution that provides the most appropriate within cluster similarities and between cluster differences. In the analysis reported here, we use a 16-cluster solution. Figure 4 shows the various identity characteristics plotted with the 16 tribes in a multiple correspondence analysis.

It is not really important to understand multiple correspondence analysis to understand the meaning of the two-dimensional plot in Figure 4. It is enough to understand that it is a plot of the various identity characteristics and the positioning of the 16 SA Tribes.

In this case, a multiple correspondence analysis has the objective of representing the relations of the tribes and the various identity characteristics in a reduced multidimensional space. Here we are looking at the first two dimensions of that space. Naming of dimensions is a somewhat subjective interpretation of more detailed output of the analysis. We would argue that the first dimension represents human development. To the left of the plot we have low human development and to the right we have high human development.

The second dimension of the plot represents things that most people have versus things that few people have. It is not possible to see such detail when the plot is reduced to fit into this page, but as the 'rainbow' curves down on the left, we have characteristics such as 'none of these things' as well as the most basic amenities such as water and electricity. To the right of the map, as the rainbow curves down, we have the luxuries such as Internet access in the home and DStv.

If we look more closely at the map, we can partition the 16 SA Tribes into four groups, as depicted in Figure 5. *Rural Survivalists* includes four tribes, *Emerging Consumers* five, *Urban Middle Class* four and *Urban Elite* includes three tribes. The balance of this chapter will briefly introduce these four general groups and I will then expand in the next chapter by looking at each of them in more detail.

Rural Survivalists

One in four (26%) South Africans are *Rural Survivalists*. *Rural Survivalists* generally live far from the major metropolitan areas of South Africa and they conduct their lives much as their grandparents conducted theirs. Some 77% of them reside in the deep rural areas. They tend to live agrarian or subsistence lifestyles, providing their own food and participating in much informal trade and barter. Almost all *Rural Survivalists* are black South Africans and traditional tribal life and customs often remain very important to them. Many live in abject poverty and about half of them could be characterised as among the poorest people in the world. Many could not survive without

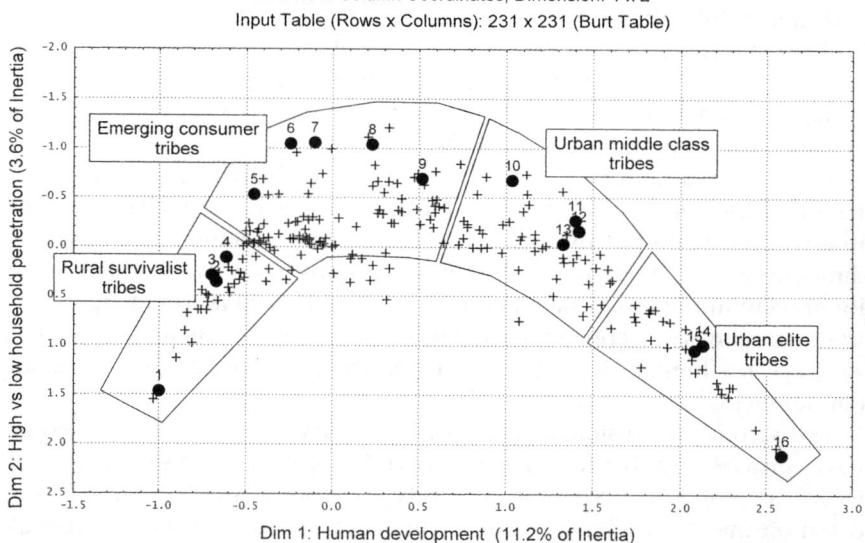

Figure 5: *The rainbow nation emerges!*

the financial support they receive from family members who are living in the metropolitan areas.

Emerging Consumers

Emerging Consumers are the largest of the four groups of SA Tribes. They comprise 39% of the South African population. They are mainly black (82%) but also include many people who refer to themselves as Coloured (16%). They are poor, but have reached a basic standard of living that includes, almost without exception, running water, electricity and a flush toilet. About half of their homes had dishwashing liquid present when the interviews were conducted. However, they are living very far from high human development. For instance, only about one in five *Emerging Consumer* homes is able to provide for its hot water needs with a geyser (hot water heater).

Urban Middle Classes

The *Urban Middle Classes* are not an urban middle class in the sense that it would be understood in Europe or America. Their household income and standard of living are much lower in comparison. Nevertheless, they have many of the amenities associated with basic human development. Almost all of them have electricity, running water, a flush toilet, a geyser and a car. More than 80% have a TV, hi-fi/music centre, fridge/freezer, telephone and microwave oven. About 1 in 5 (21%) South African homes fit into this general group.

Urban Elite

The *Urban Elite* is comprised of only three tribes and accounts for less than 8% of the country's population. It constitutes the smallest group, as measured as a proportion of the total population. Many of the *Urban Elite* live a lifestyle that would be the envy of most of the world's population – one that is equivalent in every way to that lived by their counterparts in Europe, America and the world's other richest nations. Their homes show a high state of human development. Almost two-thirds have personal computers in the home and about half of those are linked to the Internet. They experience a broad sweep of global culture through exposure to a wide range of global communications media. They are very likely to see themselves as world citizens (as well as South Africans) and compare themselves and their lifestyles to a global standard.

Conclusion

This chapter has presented a model of identity influence, explained the SA Tribes methodology and very briefly detailed four major groupings. These four are interesting in their own right. South Africa is a medium size country in terms of its economic size and population. For many products and services, these four broad classifications will comprise groups that have intrinsic value for market segmentation or service strategies. Many other products and services will want to focus on the intermarket segments[16] that are best conceptualised by focusing on the 16 individual tribes. In the following chapters we visit each of the four groupings and learn about the 16 tribes that comprise them.

4: Tribes of the new South Africa
The tribes profiled in detail

In this chapter, we take a closer look at the groups that emerged from the SA Tribes analysis by examining the basic identity characteristics of each. Each tribe is portrayed in a reasonably detailed portrait that will allow us to distinguish between them and to understand the findings that are presented in subsequent chapters, when the groups are related to behaviours of interest and where additional details are revealed.

Most marketing textbooks tell us that markets consist of people who have (a) a need, (b) financial resources and (c) the authority to spend those financial resources to satisfy their need. Even the least developed sectors of the South African market represent viable target market segments, provided that marketers are capable of finding other sources of payment such as donor agencies. Moreover, the poorer sections of society offer firms an exciting opportunity to learn about constraints under which the majority of humankind live, to develop products and services that are appropriate to their needs and develop network marketing skills that bring financial resources and market needs together.

The chapter proceeds in the following manner: each tribe is presented in order from the lowest levels of human development to the highest. We begin with the four who comprise the *Rural Survivalists*.

Rural Survivalists

Agrarian Lifestyles

In every aspect of life, on every day that they rise from sleep and stand in line waiting to receive necessary services, *Agrarian Lifestyles* have been last. In this book, at least, they will be first.

Agrarian Lifestyles are black African people living in rural areas and comprise 12.8% of the entire South African population. Thirty-five percent speak Xhosa as their home language and another 31% speak Zulu. They are dispersed geographically with 36% living in KwaZulu-Natal, 27% living in the Eastern Cape and 20% living in the Limpopo Province.

Their living circumstances are characterised by dire poverty; few people in the world experience such challenging circumstances. As a measure of their poverty, their claimed household income is approximately half of the *per capita* gross national product (an indicator of relative income per person, not per household) in Rwanda or Ethiopia, the world's two poorest countries.

Thirty-nine percent of them live in traditional huts and some 46% of all people who live in huts are part of this group. Another 34% live in shacks and 14% live in ZOZO huts. They are perhaps distinguished most by what they do not have rather than by what they have. More than 93% do not have any of the basic living standard measures: no electricity, no running water, no radio or TV, no telephone. An astounding 99.9% of all such South Africans who live in such deprived living standards – and conditions of such unacceptable human development – can be found here.

They have received very little education. Fifty-six percent have not completed primary school and 20% have received no formal education at all. So, it is little surprise that 73% of *Agrarian Lifestyles* are unemployed and 19% can find only unskilled labour positions. Three out of the four who do have jobs work full-time. Only one in three who work – 7% of the total – have an account of any kind with a bank. When asked what is most important in life, they indicate overwhelmingly that it is having a job.

So, they are poor, desperately poor. Much of their trade probably occurs in barter and the informal sector. More than two-thirds live in the lowest income level group. Eighty-four percent of all people who are measured at LSM1, the lowest level of living standard measured by SAARF, are in this tribe. LSM1 constitutes 49% of its total population; the balance is classified as LSM2 or LSM3.

There are 5.5 people in their average home and about 60% of them are women. Twenty-five percent of all people who are living together without the benefit of marriage are included in this tribe. Of these, 12% – and another 38% who are single – do not derive the benefits of marriage that accrue in South Africa. They place lowest value on stimulation and power and above average importance on tradition and conformity.

Border Survivalists

In contrast to the geographic dispersion of *Agrarian Lifestyles*, *Border Survivalists* are concentrated in the Eastern Cape province with a small proportion (13%) residing primarily in the Western Cape. They speak Xhosa in the home almost exclusively (91%). They are distinguished by their geographic concentration, but also by the high number of females (64%) and widows (17%). Thirty-eight percent of them live in traditional huts, nearly half of all such people in South Africa, and another 45% live in matchbox houses. Just more than 1% refer to themselves as Coloured.

Border Survivalists reside primarily in rural areas (69%). The 18% who live in metropolitan areas can be found in Port Elizabeth or East London. They are only marginally better educated than *Agrarian Lifestyles*, with one-third reporting not having finished primary school and 20% reporting no formal education. Although 11% say that they hold a matric or higher qualification, unemployment remains high. Eighty-six percent have no occupation, 31% are unemployed and 23% are retired. With only 18% working, household income remains low: 23% make do on R900–R1,200 and 43% on R500–R900 every month. Children are present in 70% of households and there are twice as many elderly people over 65 years of age as there are in the national sample. Their average household income of R988 must support the needs of 5.26 people.

Government has reached many of them with utilities. Three-quarters have electricity and 40% have piped water connections; 25%–50% of the homes that are connected have had services discontinued, probably because of non-payment of accounts. Telephones were present in 4% of homes but only 2% could receive calls, probably for the same reason. They are at the lowest levels of the LSM classes: LSM1 (14%), LSM2 (31%) and LSM3 (34%). None of their homes has a geyser, 10% have a flush toilet, 19% have a fridge or freezer and 27% had dishwashing liquid when the interview took place. The presence of televisions (42%) and music centres (38%) suggests that global images penetrate their lives. Eighty-four percent do not have a relationship with a bank and 95% do not have one with an insurance or assurance company. Almost all that have a relationship with a bank hold a savings account.

Border Survivalists place greater importance on conformity and security than most. Only one other tribe has a lower average optimum stimulation level. They think that having a job and an education are the two most important things in life. They place great importance on religion and their claimed religiosity on a 10-point scale is well above the national average. Fifty-nine percent claim to be members of African Christian churches. They comprise 7.2% of the South African population.

Highveld Survivalists

They are black African people who are distinguished mainly from the first two tribes by their geographic location, home language and type of housing. Comprising 14.5% of the South African population, they are the largest tribe.

Highveld Survivalists reside in the rural areas of the Limpopo Province (45%), North West Province (29%) and Mpumalanga (24%). Conversation in most homes is conducted in North Sotho (34%) or South Sotho (31%), although Tsonga or Swazi are the home language in another 22% of the households. In fact, 62% of South African Swazi-speakers and 43% of South African Tsonga-speakers can be found here. In comparison to other *Rural Survivalists*, fewer *Highveld Survivalists* reside in traditional huts. Forty-five percent live in matchbox homes. Another 18% live in improved matchbox homes or in semi-detached houses. Only 20% live in traditional huts.

Their close proximity to the industrial heartland of Africa has allowed them to be exposed to a greater degree of education. Twenty-one percent have matriculated or achieved a higher level of qualification. Ten percent report never having gone to school while 31% report that they have not completed primary school despite attending school. The portrait painted by their employment situation is as challenging as the other *Survivalists*. Forty-two percent are unemployed. Seventy-five percent report that they have no occupation. The vast majority of the 23% who are working classified their jobs as unskilled labour and one-quarter of them claim to work only part-time.

Forty-three percent of respondents reported that they were married or living together as a couple. Fifty-one percent are single. Children are present in 69% of households. As with the other survivalist groups, economic resources are severely stretched. Twenty-three percent of households survive on less than R500 per month and 58% on R900 per month or less. In such severely challenged circumstances, it is no surprise that 84% do not have a relationship with a bank and 94% do not have a relationship with any other type of financial institution. Those who have an account, have a savings account. Five percent have a funeral policy.

Living standards reflect the challenging economic circumstances. About half of the homes are hooked up to electricity and water but about 20% of those connections are not being used, probably because of non-payment. Twenty-three percent of homes have flush toilets. Fridge/freezers (6%), TVs (19%), music centres (13%) and cars (2%) are present in some homes but not widely possessed. Not one home has a geyser, microwave oven, vacuum cleaner/floor polisher or cellphone. Telkom has reached 1%.

Their values and personality traits are not distinctive. They place high importance on conservation and self-transcendence values and low importance on openness to change and self-enhancement. They want jobs and education.

KZN Survivalists

KZN Survivalists are black African shack-dwellers who reside in rural KwaZulu-Natal. They speak Zulu in the home (South Sotho, 6%) and most practise some form of Christianity. Religion distinguishes them somewhat from the other *Survivalists*; some 20% are Roman Catholic. Like the other *Survivalists*, the largest number report belonging to an African Christian church. Fifty-four percent are single and 32% are married. Children are present in 88% of households. They are a large group comprising 8.2% of the total South African population.

Fifty-four percent live in shacks and another 21% in ZOZO huts. Almost all of the 13% who reside near a metropolitan area live in the outlying areas of Durban. Some 13% have matriculated or achieved a higher qualification, but 45% have not finished primary school. Ten percent have never had any formal education. So, once again, we see the same challenged circumstances for employment. Four out of ten people are unemployed. Eight out of ten report that they have no occupation. Of the 36% who do work, about four out of ten work part-time.

They have achieved the highest standard of living of the four survivalist tribes – 46% are classified as LSM4 or LSM5 – but it is no privileged existence. Not one home had a geyser, and only 5% had a flush toilet. Thirteen percent had dishwashing liquid on hand when interviewed. About half of the homes have a television and/or music centre. Ten percent have a motor car and/or telephone. Sixty-five percent of homes have electricity and water is piped to 39%. Almost every home that has utility connections reported that they were in working order.

KZN Survivalists want jobs, education and a higher standard of living more than anything else. Their optimum stimulation level does not differ from the national average. They are distinguished by the high importance they place on conformity. They place very low importance on hedonism. Their ratings of universalism and tradition are lower than might be expected for a survivalist. They place less importance on *living in freedom* and *living in a country that is free* than the national average.

As a group, *Rural Survivalists* share the common characteristics of dire poverty and low human development. They are among the poorest people in the world. The small amount of money that is available is stretched to provide the basic necessities of life. High unemployment and lack of prospects suggest that they spend much of their days trying to find ways to fill life's basic needs and pass the time. We now move on to the *Emerging Consumers*.

Emerging consumers
Free State Emerging

Free State Emerging comprises 5.2% of the South African population. Although it represents a group of black African people who live in economically challenging circumstances, *Free State Emerging* can be differentiated from the *Rural Survivalists* in almost every way. First, the majority reside primarily in cities or large towns (35%) and metropolitan areas (7% in Bloemfontein) located in the Free State. Only 36% reside in rural areas. Although 21% reside in shacks, 77% live in a matchbox home, RDP house or suburban neighbourhood. Half are single and the balance is primarily married. Eleven percent are widowed and children are present in 57% of homes.

Fifty-five percent report that they belong to an African Christian church and 23% are Roman Catholics. Nevertheless, they rate their religiosity (2.98) lowest of any tribe on a 10-point scale. This is somewhat surprising given that 17% are over 65 years of age and the average age of respondents was nearly 40.

They have been deprived access to good education. One-third has not completed primary school and 12% report no formal education. Work is scarce and, as was the case with the *Rural Survivalists*, almost all report that they have no occupation (87%). Forty-one percent report that they are unemployed, as opposed to out of work because of other reasons such as retirement. Eight percent work in trades or semi-skilled positions. Of the 22% who work, 41% work part-time.

They are much less challenged than their *Rural Survivalist* counterparts. Almost every home has electricity (95%) and water (87%) connections, although a much smaller proportion have electricity (50%) or water (18%) laid on at present, probably because of non-payment. Fifty-two percent of homes get by on more than R900 per month and 59% are classified as LSM4 or LSM5. Over half of the homes have a television, flush toilet and/or fridge/freezer. Thirty-five percent had dishwashing liquid present when interviewed, 43% had a music centre, 16% a Telkom phone, 5% had a car and 2% had geysers or microwave ovens. Nevertheless, washing machines, vacuum cleaners/floor polishers, DStv, cellphones, the Internet and personal computers were not found in any of these homes. Only 16% have a relationship with a bank and less than half that number has another type of financial relationship.

The members of *Free State Emerging* want to have a job more than anything else in life. They are among the least likely to want *a world without war* or *religion*. They place the greatest value on self-transcendence and conservation values. They are distinguished by the highest reported optimum stimulation level of all the groups.

Matchbox Suburban Youth

Matchbox Suburban Youth is a large group of black African people who are dispersed widely throughout South Africa. One-third speaks Zulu in the home and one-quarter speaks Tswana. Given their language preference, it is not surprising that the majority reside in KwaZulu-Natal (27%) and the North West Province (24%). Nevertheless, substantial populations can be found in Mpumalanga, the Limpopo Province and the Eastern Cape. Only 19% live in rural areas. Almost the same numbers reside in major metropolitan areas. The majority live in large cities, small cities and towns outside the major metropolitan areas. They are primarily members of African Christian churches (48%), Protestant churches (22%) and the Roman Catholic Church (14%).

They are distinguished by their youth – their average age is only 26 – and single marital status (86%). Children are present in 83% of homes. Sixty-eight percent are less than 24 years of age and only 7% are older than 45. Sixty-one percent have some high school and 25% have matriculated or achieved a higher qualification. They are more likely than any other tribe to report that they have no occupation, which is not surprising as 46% are still in school.

They are less economically challenged than the groups discussed earlier. Only 36% earn less than R900 per month and 18% report household income exceeds R2,500. Most are either too young to bank or are unemployed, so it is not surprising that 88% are 'unbanked' and 97% are 'unassured'.

Their standard of living is much higher than previous groups and there is evidence that items associated with a higher standard of living have begun to penetrate these homes. Only 9% live in shacks, with three-quarters living in matchbox homes and the balance in suburban homes. Nearly every home has electricity and water connections, and at least 90% of the connections were working on the day of the interview. Seventy-one percent are classified as LSM5, LSM6 or LSM7. Eighty-seven percent of homes have a TV, 79% have a flush toilet and/or fridge/freezer, 73% have a music centre and 33% have a Telkom telephone. Between 4% and 12% of homes have a car, microwave oven, washing machine, vacuum cleaner/floor polisher or cellular telephone.

Matchbox Suburban Youth thinks a job is the most important thing in life and rates religion much lower than the national average. Although they are not their most important values, its members rate power, achievement and hedonism much higher than others. They have the second highest optimum stimulation level and comprise 9.0% of South Africans.

Gauteng Township Youth

This group is distinguished by its geographic location in the townships of Gauteng major metropolitan areas. Although 31% speak Zulu in the home, they are black Africans who speak the full spectrum of indigenous languages. Their religious preferences are similar to *Matchbox Suburban Youth*, with the exception that 20% claim to have no religion. Their reported religiosity is also well below the national average.

Their average age is a young 37 years and 51% are single. Forty-one percent are married or living together. Some 25% have not completed primary school but an equal proportion have matriculated. The majority have had some high school education. Forty-three percent are unemployed – more than any other group – and 75% claim they have no occupation. Those who find work find it in the unskilled and semi-skilled areas. As a result, household income is not particularly impressive, but good as compared to previous groups. Only 28% earn less than R900 per month. Five percent earn more than R5,000. Children are present in 68% of homes but the average number of people per home is among the lowest at 4.78, leaving R1,769 per month on average to serve their needs.

The living standard of this group compares favourably with previous groups. Almost every home has electricity and water supplied, but the water was not presently hooked up in 39% of homes. Seventy-nine percent are classified as LSM5, LSM6 or LSM7. Eighty-nine percent have flush toilets, 78% have TV, 74% have a fridge/freezer, 50% have music centres and approximately 10–15% have a car, microwave oven, washing machine or geyser. MNet was present in 1% of these homes and twice that number had a cellular telephone. Twenty-seven percent have a relationship with a bank but only 7% have a relationship with another financial institution.

Gauteng Township Youth believes that a job and education are the most important things in life; it places much higher importance on achievement than other groups, even though it is not its most important value. Its members place less relative importance than other groups on self-transcendence and conservation values – despite rating these as their most important values. At a score of 20.2, only five other groups surpass their optimum stimulation level. They comprise 9.7% of the total South African population.

Cape Coloured Emerging

Its members are distinguished by their almost exclusive description of themselves as Coloured (98%), their Afrikaans home language (94%), their domicile in the Western Cape (75%) and Eastern Cape (15%) and their religiosity – which ranks among the top five tribes. They are primarily Christians, with 40% claiming to be Protestants and 7% claiming to follow Islam.

They reside in urban areas in the main with only 20% living in rural areas. About half can be found in the periphery of a major metropolitan area, mainly Cape Town. Two-thirds live in matchbox houses or suburban homes. Nine percent live in a flat and 22% live in a semi-detached home, the highest incidence for any tribe in both cases. Forty-six percent of respondents are single, 39% are married and children are present in 81% of their homes.

Cape Coloured Emerging is better educated, but many of its members still have not matriculated in most cases. Forty-eight percent have completed some high school and 14% have matriculated or achieved a higher qualification. Still, despite their urban domicile, 23% have not completed primary school. Their average household income is R2,091 and 30% earn between R1,400 and R3,000 monthly, the highest incidence of all tribes. Sixty-six percent claim to have no occupation but 46% are working, 34% full-time. Those who work generally hold unskilled and semi-skilled jobs.

Sixty percent are living at LSM6 or LSM7; only 21% live at LSM4 or below. Electricity (97%) and water (98%) are connected and on (91% and 84%) in almost every house. Forty-six percent of homes have a Telkom telephone and 89% of those phones were working. More than 80% of homes have flush toilets, TVs and fridge/freezers. Washing machines (50%), music centres (51%), dishwashing liquid (69%) and geysers (33%) are common. Cellphones and MNet reach about 10%.

Cape Coloured Emerging has a high optimum stimulation level, ranking fourth among all the groups. They say that a job is most important and place more importance on achieving a good standard of living when compared to the others. This is somewhat in contrast to the relatively low value they place on power, achievement, hedonism, stimulation and self-direction. They place above average importance on self-transcendence and conservation values. They are 5.1% of all South Africans.

Prime Skills

The *Prime Skills* group is distinguished by its proximity to the *Urban Middle Class*, upon whose door it is knocking. Its constituents are black African people in the thirties and forties who generally speak an Nguni home language (but who include speakers of all indigenous black African languages) and live in major metropolitan areas and other urban areas scattered throughout South Africa. Sixty percent of respondents were males and 83% of their households had children present.

Prime Skills' most distinguishing characteristic is its relatively high education and high level of employment. Seventy-one percent are working, 15% are professionals and 45% are working in skilled or semi-skilled positions. Only 14% are unemployed. Their average household income of R3,151 leaves R822 per person in the median (middle) household.

Their standard of living is approaching middle class. Almost all are connected to electricity and water utilities and it is working in 87% and 75% of homes, respectively. Only 3% do not have a bank account of some kind and only 30% fail to have an assurance or insurance policy. One in five households has purchased a durable item on credit in the last year. One-third have a funeral or whole life policy. Almost half have reached LSM7 or LSM8 and 86% are at LSM6 or above. Fridge/freezers (96%), TVs (94%), flush toilets (89%), music centres (85%) and dishwashing liquid are common. Geysers (34%), cars (30%), microwave ovens (24%), washing machines (20%) and cellphones (11%) are less common but much more widespread than in previous tribes.

It is a Christian group that rates its religiosity among the highest of any of the groups. They are active participants in religion, reporting that they practise religion more frequently than most others. They place more importance, relatively, on achievement than the national average and less importance on benevolence. Their optimum stimulation level is near the national average. They comprise 6.7% of the total South African population.

Considered as a group of tribes, *Emerging Consumers* are characterised by a life that often entails much financial hardship, careful budgeting for some luxury items, and freedom from worry about day-to-day survival. The family is very important and the social network of relations is generally well looked after. In contrast, the *Urban Middle Class* has reached a higher standard of living that allows its members to consider other value priorities, but also to encounter psychosocial forces that tear at the family and individual.

Urban Middle Class

East Coast Settlers

This is one of the smallest groups, comprising just 2.7% of the South African population. Its constituents are distinguished by their ethnicity and religious beliefs. They are people who speak English exclusively in the home, describe themselves as Indian (78%), Coloured (14%) or white (8%) and reside primarily in large metropolitan areas (81%), especially Durban (57%). They are primarily Hindu (42%), Christian (37%) and Muslim (19%).

Half describe themselves as having completed some high school, 30% have matriculated and another 6% have acquired a tertiary qualification. An equal proportion of the respondents (21%) were under 25 years of age and over 55. Two-thirds are married, 22% are single and children are present in 66% of homes. Their family size is relatively small compared to the others (4.5 people).

East Coast Settlers have achieved a true South African middle-class standard of living, with a household income of R5,421 per month. Eight percent earn more than R10,000 per month and only 6% earn less than R1,200. Eighty-seven percent are classified as LSM7 or LSM8. Nearly every household has electricity, water, a telephone, fridge/freezer, TV, music centre, flush toilet, geyser, microwave oven and dishwashing liquid. The large incidence of an 'unbanked' population – 40% have no relationship with a bank and 57% have no relationship with another financial institution – is somewhat surprising. Those that do have an account have a wide spectrum of accounts. There is evidence of adoption of innovative financial services: cheque accounts, retirement annuities and credit cards have penetrated this market equally but have not been adopted widely (7%).

Their optimum stimulation level is among the lowest of all the tribes. They place above average importance on conservation and self-transcendence values.

The Believers

The Believers are mainly white people (91%) but include people of all races. They speak either Afrikaans (72%) or English (28%) in the home. They are distinguished by their religious beliefs. Fifty-two percent believe that *being faithful to one's religion* is the most important thing in life and another 38% believe that a happy family is the most important thing. Although they rate their religiosity lower than all but two groups, they engage in religious practice more frequently than any other. With the exception of the 1% that is Muslim, they are affiliated with Christian churches and include the second highest proportion of Protestants (52%). They comprise 3.5% of the total population.

The Believers are older people who reside mainly in suburban homes (80%), with the balance residing in granny flats, flats and townhouses.

Although 85% are resident in urban areas, only 42% are in the major metropolitan areas. They are widely spread across South Africa. Fifty-six percent are over the age of 55. Sixty-four percent of the respondents were male, 26% were homemakers and only 38% were working. They are primarily married (61%) or widowed (22%). Children were present in 33% of the households, which are comprised of only 3.1 people on average.

The standard of living is comfortable but not extravagant. All but 4% are classified as LSM7 or LSM8. All of the basic measures of living standard are found in their homes – dishwashing liquid, flush toilet, geyser, fridge/freezer, TV, washing machine. MNet and cellular phones have penetrated about one-third of these homes; about 10% have a portable computer and/or DStv. Three percent report Internet connections in the home. They have 1.24 cars per household and 82% have telephones. They are sophisticated users of basic financial service products but few take out loans (4%). Whole life assurance, retirement annuities, funeral policies, short-term insurance and medical insurance are held in 15%–20% of these homes. Thirty-eight percent have domestic help.

The Believers place high value on conformity, tradition, security, universalism and benevolence. They are among the least likely to choose education as the most important thing in life. Their mean optimum stimulation level ranks lowest of all the tribes, suggesting that they dislike change.

Suburban Bliss

Suburban Bliss represents a group of young people of all races who live in suburban homes and comprise 3.6% of the total population. Describing their race as white (67%), Coloured (27%), black (5%) or Asian (2%), its members are distinguished by their youth (mean age 20.3), their domicile (a suburban home, 84%) and high household income (mean R10,370 per month). They generally have had some high school (44%) or have matriculated (46%); many were still in high school at the time of the interview. Ninety-four percent were single and 56% were below the age of 20.

Constituents of *Suburban Bliss* reside in every major city, with Cape Town (24%) and Johannesburg (11%) the two places they are most likely to call home. There are 4.34 people in the average home and 47% include children. They are primarily students (55%) but one-third are working, mainly in semi-skilled positions. It is not surprising that they are financially unsophisticated – most are too young to attract any attention from a bank or financial institution – but 71% have a savings account and 30% have already acquired an assurance or insurance product of some kind.

Suburban Bliss homes are well appointed with all of the basic indicators of living standard achievement and high human development. There are 1.9 cars per household and 65% are classified as LSM8. The balance is classified as LSM7. MNet and cellular phones have penetrated nearly two-thirds of households, DStv 13% and home Internet access is available in 21% of homes.

Their youth explains their high optimum stimulation level. They like new and novel things and enjoy the pleasures of life. They place higher value on hedonism than any of the other groups and place second on stimulation. Self-direction and benevolence are also important values for them. Although they are well off now, they realise it is because of their parents' success and they believe a job and education are the two most important things in life.

Suburban Challenge

The members of this group are in perhaps the most stressful years of life: 68% are between the ages of 25–34 and three-quarters are between 20 and 34. They are primarily white (70%) but also describe themselves as Coloured (18%), black (8%) and Asian (5%). They speak English (49%) and Afrikaans (43%) primarily in the home. Forty-two percent are married and 36% are single. Children are present in 62% of homes. This group comprises just 2.6% of the total population.

Suburban Challenge constituents rate their religiosity higher than most groups and are among the most likely to have performed some religious practice today. Primarily Christian, they also include a few Muslims (2%) and Jews (1%). Fourteen percent of all Jewish people surveyed can be found in this group.

They are well educated and upwardly mobile. Not one person in this group has failed to attend high school and 64% have matriculated or achieved a higher qualification. Eleven percent have a technical diploma of some kind. Seventy-three percent are working, almost all full-time, and the need for faster economic growth becomes very apparent when it is seen that as many as 12% are unemployed in a group such as this. Their upward mobility comes at a price: 14% report that they are divorced, more than any other group.

Their education and work allows them to enjoy a relatively high standard of living. They reside in suburban homes (71%) for the most part, but also in matchbox houses (12%), flats (6%) and semi-detached houses (5%). Sixty-five percent of homes are classified as LSM8 and 99% as LSM7 or LSM8; two or three percent fail to have some of the basic indicators of a good living standard. More advanced indicators of living standard achievement, such as a vacuum cleaner/floor polisher or microwave oven, can be found in eight of ten homes. There are 1.3 cars per household. Ten percent of homes have Internet connections and 16% have personal computers. There are more homes with cellular phones (55%) than Telkom phones (50%).

They are financially sophisticated and hold a wide range of accounts. Only 11% do not have a bank account and only 30% fail to have another type of relationship with a financial institution. Twenty-one percent have cheque accounts and 14% have credit cards. Twenty-eight percent have a whole life policy, 22% an endowment policy and 19% hold a funeral policy.

The most important thing in life, from their perspective, is a job. They were much less likely than other groups to say that a *country free of war* was the most important thing. They are characterised by the higher relative importance they place on openness to change values. Stimulation, hedonism and self-direction are relatively more important to them than others. They place much lower importance on conformity. They have the third highest optimum stimulation level of any group.

Thus, the *Urban Middle Class* enjoys a comfortable life and is a ready market for most goods. We now move on to the *Urban Elite*.

Urban Elite

Earth Mothers

At first glance, they are 2.7% of the total population who are somewhat difficult to categorise. They are white (83%), Coloured (16%) and Asian (1%). So, one could say they are not black. They are principally Christian but include Muslims (2%), Hindus (1%) and Jews (3%). In fact, 38% of all Jewish people are in this tribe but that is not really helpful either. Their religiosity and frequency of religious practice scores are above average. So is their education: almost half have a post-matric qualification. They are scattered in the major urban centres; a third of them call Cape Town home. Nevertheless, none of these observations really captures their differences from the others.

They are distinguished by their home language and value priorities. Ninety-nine percent speak English in the home. They place an abnormally high importance on self-transcendence values. Other people, close and distant, animals and the environment are important to them. In the next chapter, we see that this value orientation is an important indicator of their lifestyle interests as well. They place little relative importance on openness to change values and their optimum stimulation level is among the lowest of all the tribes.

The *Earth Mothers* are among the oldest of the 16 tribes. Forty-seven percent are over the age of 50. Seventy-eight percent are married and 57% are female. Twenty-six percent are retired and almost half say they have no occupation. Clerical work (17%) and the trades (12%) are popular choices for the 52% who do work. Their household is among the smallest of all groups, including only 3.23 people on average.

Like all *Urban Elite* tribes, they enjoy a standard of living that is equivalent to that experienced in the most developed nations. Their average household income is R10,670. Ninety-three percent are classified as LSM8. Fifty-eight percent employ a domestic helper in the home. There are nearly two cars per household. Every indicator of living standard is present in most homes. MNet is in 60% of homes, DStv in 14%, personal computers in 60% and one-third have Internet access.

Family Focus

They are a small group (2.4% of the population) comprised of Afrikaans-speaking (87%) whites (97%) who are distinguished by religiosity, education, age and high human development but, more importantly, by their focus on the family. Openness to change, stimulation in particular, is unimportant. Universalism is not particularly important. One would expect this to suggest that benevolence would also be of average importance but this is not so. Only three other groups rate benevolence – which is of course focused on concern and caring for the family and others who are near and dear – higher than does *Family Focus*.

Family Focus rates its religiosity higher than any other group and is Christian, almost without exception. Its members are the second most likely to engage in frequent religious practice. However, it is very possible that their religiosity is directed towards those close to them. It is also possible that a phrase such as 'love thy neighbour' applies to a much more limited subset of people than it would to others, especially *Rural Survivalists* and *Emerging Consumers*. Their optimum stimulation level is near the national average.

They are the third oldest group (average age 43 years). Only 9% have not acquired a matriculation qualification and one-third hold a post-matric qualification.

Their occupational profile is unique. Sixty-seven percent are working, almost all full-time. They have the second highest proportion of self-employed (11%) and third highest proportion of executives (11%). Twenty-one percent work in clerical or sales positions. This provides them with an average income of R13,480 and one in seven households earns more than R26,000 per month.

Such a high standard of commercial success allows them to enjoy a very high standard of living. Ninety-four percent of *Family Focus* households are classified as LSM8 and there are 1.79 cars per household. The basic and advanced indicators of living standards can be found in just about every home. MNet and cellular telephones are in more than 70% of homes. Despite their older age, one in six homes is connected to the Internet.

They exhibit much financial sophistication: not one of them says that they do not have a relationship with a bank and another type of financial institution. Eighty-eight percent have cheque accounts, 70% credit cards, 40% investment accounts and 46% petroleum cards. More than three-quarters have a whole life policy, endowment, retirement annuity and/or short-term insurance policy.

Achievers

Their standard of living is the highest in South Africa. Accounting for just 2.7% of the population, they live a life of material ease compared to others. They are primarily white people (91%) who speak Afrikaans (72%) or English (28%) in the home and reside in a suburban home (93%) located in a major metropolitan area. They are scattered across South Africa. Thirty-five percent live in the Western Cape with substantial populations also residing in the Free State (18%) and Gauteng (16%).

Achievers are distinguished by educational attainments that would be the envy of people anywhere in the world. One-quarter has graduated from university and 4% have a professional qualification. In fact, one in seven South African professionals is a member of this group. Anyone who needs proof of the power of innovation and entrepreneurship needs look no further: one in five of the nation's self-employed can be found here.

Their educational and commercial attainments allow *Achievers* to enjoy a standard of living enjoyed by few people in the world. Given the rand/dollar exchange rate, their average household income of R16,200 may not seem very impressive but it allows them to afford every basic and advanced indicator of living standard measured by SA Tribes.

It is a lifestyle characterised by all of the modern technical advances and conveniences. Two-thirds of households have personal computers and half of them are connected to the Internet. Two-thirds also have MNet and 27% have DStv. There are 2.1 cars per household, 89% have a cellular telephone and 88% a Telkom phone.

Their value priorities are unique. They place higher importance on self-direction than any other tribe. Benevolence is also of vital importance. Power and hedonism are generally more important to them than others, but do not rise to a higher level than what could be called moderate importance. Conservation values are also moderately important, which is interesting considering that their power over others would cause them to value it in others while their need to be innovative and lead would encourage them to place less importance on it.

Over half of *Achievers* indicate that *being faithful to one's religion* and *to have a happy family life* are the most important things in life. Although they rate their religiosity on a 10-point scale much lower than the national average, they are the second most likely to engage in prayer, attend church or engage in another religious practice. Probably because they have it and cannot conceive of losing it, they are among the least likely to choose *to have a good standard of living* as the most important thing in life. Their optimum stimulation level is relatively high, placing them fifth among the 16 tribes.

Conclusion

This chapter has presented a textual portrait of each tribe. As might be expected after so many decades of so-called 'separate development', they are differentiated mainly by living standard, geography, race and ethnicity. The *Urban Elite* and the *Rural Survivalists* may often reside in areas that are separated by a short drive, but it is obvious that they live in worlds that are separated by far more. In fact, it is difficult to believe that either tribe understands the other very well. It is one thing to speak of historical disadvantage and quite another to understand it. Similarly, it is very easy to characterise the suburban lifestyles of the *Urban Elite* as a stress-free paradise where people lie by the swimming pool all day. National unity requires overcoming the inaccurate perceptions of socially distant people, as are so commonly found in South Africa. This is a task that presents government policymakers with a challenge of incredible complexity.

For those who wish to serve the needs of these various people, it is important to understand their worldview and needs. The *Rural Survivalists* have the most basic of needs and they constitute 26% of the population. Living as they do, in such deprived circumstances, they are historic victims awaiting a change to a promised better life. They need massive intervention to raise their standard of living, which must be conducted in consultation with them. Self-help, small enterprise and other educational programmes are of special appeal, especially those directed at women in this community. Companies that can develop the necessary competencies required to interest local and foreign funding sources and persuade them to become involved in upliftment programmes will find a ready market for their services.

Emerging Consumers represent a different kind of opportunity. They are beyond survival needs but struggle in difficult economic circumstances. Here the focus needs to be on consolidating and improving individual and community skills and uplifting the standard of living. Although the same type of programmes may be needed in many cases, the goal will frequently be to empower people with a very basic education in order to attain a higher set of skills that will make them employable. Firms should study this group carefully. They are not only the largest group in South Africa, they also share many characteristics with the largest groups in the developing world. South African Breweries is perhaps the best example of the global competitiveness in Eastern Europe, Asia and other fast-growing regions that accrues to a firm that understands this market well.

The *Urban Middle Class* shows signs of coping with rapid social, political and economic change. They live at the edge of the consumer society. They are coping in different ways. Religion, family and caring for those near and dear are very important. However, the high divorce rate is indicative of the high levels of social stress and it may well be that there is a need to pay particular attention to their psychosocial needs. Companies would do well to understand the diffusion of innovations in this group. They are now reaching a point where they can afford what many South Africans consider to be luxuries. It is important for firms to understand how they will acquire products and in what order, so they can target them for marketing activities at the right time.

The *Urban Elite* represent a different set of needs and opportunities. Most are settled and happy but it is likely that many of them compare their standard of living to global peers on a much more regular basis than previously. Many have friends and family who have emigrated and one could expect that many are experiencing doubts about the long-term stability of their residence in South Africa, especially the young. For the government, this means maintaining the so-called first-world infrastructure of South Africa (which again requires a great balancing act). It is vitally important that schools, roads, hospitals and the like deliver acceptable levels of service and care and that young people feel that South Africa will have a place for them. To some extent, this means informing the public about the levels of service and care delivered in the countries where people are most likely to wish to emigrate. The commercial reality of this tribe is well known. There is little doubt that this is a sector of the population that has much appeal to marketers of advanced products.

It is one thing to present a list of new tribes and bury the reader in detail. But it is quite another to show the importance of understanding the groups. In the next chapter, we explore two outcomes of understanding tribal identity by linking it to brand preferences and to lifestyle interests.

5: Consumer behaviour
How you do the washing says a lot about who you think you are

Having presented a portrait of the 16 SA Tribes, we now demonstrate the power of identity in predicting people's purchase and consumption choices. In this chapter we present two types of results. First, we examine some typical lifestyle interests that people have and link them to SA Tribes' findings. The tribes differ significantly on all of the 40 lifestyle interests we measured.[1] We explore seven of those interests here to demonstrate the kind of differences that emerge.

Marketers are most interested in two types of behaviour: product category participation and brand choice. They want to know who buys products such as theirs and who buys their brand. Although we were unable to gain permission to show the results of brand preferences from sponsors – understandably because such information has great competitive value – Markinor has allowed us to publish results that we released in an earlier SA Tribes study in which we identified 14 tribes. We present those results later in the chapter in order to demonstrate the power of identity in understanding brand choice. The results in the product category (cigarette brands) are not the most impressive that we could present if we had gained permission. Moreover, we have achieved similar results for the 16 tribes presented in this book.

Identity and lifestyle interests

Lifestyle is a summary characteristic of people that includes activities, interests and opinions. In Chapter 7, Mari Harris joins me to discuss our findings concerning political party affiliations and political opinion. In the current chapter, we explore several interests: books (fiction), records/ tapes/CDs, health and fitness, women's clothing and gardening.

Books (fiction)
Works of fiction could be termed 'time-using goods'.[2] They have the capacity to occupy one's leisure hours and transport one mentally to another place. In this sense, fiction can also be thought of as a tool for escaping stress

and tension-filled environments. In the same sense, fiction may act as a substitute for travel when people lack the necessary resources. However, none of these benefits is available to someone who cannot read, find a book in a language they can read or afford to buy a book.

Table 5 illustrates the claimed interest in fiction by each of the tribes. It is clear that interest climbs with each progressive group. *Emerging Consumers* have an interest that is about the same as the national average of 13.8%. The *Urban Elite* are two or three times as likely to be interested as the national average.

Table 5: *Interest in fiction*

Agrarian Lifestyles	Border Survivalists	Highveld Survivalists	KZN Survivalists	
3.4%	2.6%	7.2%	4.7%	
Free State Emerging	Matchbox Suburban Youth	Gauteng Township Youth	Cape Coloured Emerging	Prime Skills
13.9%	14.9%	12.9%	15.5%	16.3%
East Coast Settlers	The Believers	Suburban Bliss	Suburban Challenge	
21.2%	33.9%	32.8%	25.0%	
Earth Mothers	Family Focus	Achievers		National Average
44.7%	33.2%	30.2%		13.8%

Records, tapes and CDs

Records, tapes and CDs also have the capacity to serve as a time-using good, to provide momentary escape and elevate one's mood. Music fits anyone's language and, although one needs to have equipment to play it, one can have much interest even when the budget is prohibitive.

Table 6: *Interest in records, tapes and CDs*

Agrarian Lifestyles	Border Survivalists	Highveld Survivalists	KZN Survivalists	
24.4%	25.5%	37.4%	26.7%	
Free State Emerging	Matchbox Suburban Youth	Gauteng Township Youth	Cape Coloured Emerging	Prime Skills
46.8%	50.9%	50.1%	47.6%	45.7%
East Coast Settlers	The Believers	Suburban Bliss	Suburban Challenge	
34.4%	35.7%	73.2%	59.1%	
Earth Mothers	Family Focus	Achievers		National Average
43.1%	40.8%	52.6%		40.5%

Music is an age-related product, but the pattern that emerges also shows much less interest from the *Rural Survivalists*; this is to be expected because in many cases they cannot afford to buy the products or the necessary equipment. Had we asked about interest in radio, we might expect a very different pattern to emerge. It is also important to consider that the relatively stable interest across all the groups in records, tapes and CDs hides probable variations in interest from one artist to another.

Health and fitness

Health and fitness offers obvious benefits to everyone. Although methods for attaining health and fitness may differ dramatically between the groups, we can expect all to be interested in these things. And they are, as Table 7 shows.

Table 7: *Interest in health and fitness*

Agrarian Lifestyles	Border Survivalists	Highveld Survivalists	KZN Survivalists	
30.1%	49.7%	49.5%	40.6%	
Free State Emerging	Matchbox Suburban Youth	Gauteng Township Youth	Cape Coloured Emerging	Prime Skills
62.9%	58.6%	55.1%	36.0%	68.2%
East Coast Settlers	The Believers	Suburban Bliss	Suburban Challenge	
49.3%	42.8%	53.6%	54.1%	
Earth Mothers	Family Focus	Achievers		National Average
51.5%	38.8%	61.1%		49.2%

There are some important deviations from the national average. The lowly Agrarian Lifestyles, struggling as they do on the very edge of survival, indicate the least interest in health and fitness. It is no surprise that Family Focus, the eldest group, would also be less interested. However, given their relatively high optimum stimulation level, the result for Cape Coloured Emerging is important, indicating perhaps a cultural norm that favours less emphasis on health and fitness.

Women's clothing

As we noted in the opening chapter, clothes communicate identity. They tell others much about how we feel and what we think. Interest in fashion could

Table 8: *Interest in women's clothing*

Agrarian Lifestyles	Border Survivalists	Highveld Survivalists	KZN Survivalists	
53.4%	57.0%	67.1%	43.2%	
Free State Emerging	Matchbox Suburban Youth	Gauteng Township Youth	Cape Coloured Emerging	Prime Skills
68.2%	55.9%	56.9%	42.7%	65.6%
East Coast Settlers	The Believers	Suburban Bliss	Suburban Challenge	
48.4%	41.6%	38.7%	34.0%	
Earth Mothers	Family Focus	Achievers		National Average
36.5%	32.6%	27.4%		53.2%

be a driving force behind someone's interest in women's clothing. Being fashionably dressed suggests achievement and social acceptance. The high price of fashion makes it unaffordable and aspirational for many people in the lower economic strata of society. Many people dream of being able to afford an elegant shirt of the kind worn by Madiba or a dress of the type worn at the high society functions publicised in the newspapers and magazines of the day. Interest in women's clothing can also be motivated by the desire to take care of one's family, or to live more comfortably or less expensively.

People develop an interest in things that they do not have and want; things that they have but want to improve; things that they have and want to keep. We expect as a result that women's clothing would be more important to the more economically challenged groups and of least importance to the *Urban Elite*, who can easily afford whatever clothing they may need.

The expected pattern emerges, as shown in Table 8. The *Achievers* place half as much importance on women's clothing as the national average and interest peaks in the most economically challenged groups.

Gardening

It is also important to realise that the inability to attain something in one's own life does not necessarily imply that one would not have an interest in it. Gardening can be a satisfying, peaceful and liberating experience for many people but hard work for others. Gardening does require time and money. If one considers, on one hand, the deprived financial circumstances of the *Rural Survivalists* or, on the other hand, the limited time resources of

Table 9: *Interest in gardening*

Agrarian Lifestyles	Border Survivalists	Highveld Survivalists	KZN Survivalists	
50.7%	49.6%	46.5%	44.2%	
Free State Emerging	Matchbox Suburban Youth	Gauteng Township Youth	Cape Coloured Emerging	Prime Skills
66.2%	36.4%	43.6%	42.6%	41.5%
East Coast Settlers	The Believers	Suburban Bliss	Suburban Challenge	
45.0%	51.3%	21.8%	40.2%	
Earth Mothers	Family Focus	Achievers		National Average
56.0%	55.0%	49.2%		45.9%

the *Urban Elite*, then one might wonder if such groups could be interested in gardening. However, by taking on the perspective of social identity and the SA Tribes, it is possible that the former might consider it to be a characteristic aspect of a life that they cannot attain; the latter might consider it an aspiration that can be attained, so long as others can be employed to do the more time-consuming tasks.

The results confirm our hypotheses, as shown in Table 9. *Suburban Bliss*, with its high optimum stimulation level, has little interest in gardening. Other groups do not diverge much from the national average.

Summary of lifestyle interests

We can then conclude that we can reliably predict patterns of interest among the 16 tribes. In some cases, interest will increase along with the increasing human development of each group. Home computing, small business computing, collectibles and handicrafts are interests that show increasing significance as we move along the SA Tribes rainbow, from low to high human development. In other cases – such as women's clothing, jewellery and fashion accessories, photography and education – an opposite pattern will emerge in a predictable way. In yet still other cases, a characteristic such as optimum stimulation level – rather than human development or financial or time resources – will help us understand why groups will or will not have endorsed a particular lifestyle interest. Stamp collecting, as a substititute for international travel and a way of attaining novel experiences, is one such interest – despite its image in many people's minds as a rather different activity. We now turn our attention to brand choice.

Identity and brand choice

If you were asked to pretend for a moment that Coca-Cola was a person and then asked to describe that person, chances are you would describe someone young, active and full of excitement. Johnson's Baby Shampoo might be a little girl, probably with blonde hair. Vodacom would be a black 'Yebo, Gogo' man with a sense of humour and a sparkle in his eye. It is common cause that consumer brands have personalities that reflect on our identity and say something about us.[3] They tell the world whether we are 'cool', conservative, aspiring or content. Some brands communicate exclusivity. Others become known as 'people's brands' and communicate inclusivity.

Brand choice was one of the first things we examined in the SA Tribes programme. In this section, we present the 14-cluster solution that was presented at the Association for Consumer Research Conference in 1999, and which later appeared in the American journal *Advances in Consumer Research*.[4] We proceed in the following manner. First, we briefly explore the identity of the 14 groups and attempt to understand better what leads them to emerge from the analysis. Next, we discuss the methodology we used to detect the link between these preliminary groups and cigarette brand choice. We examine two aspects of the way people choose and use brands. We look at the link with brands they have used at any time in the past. We then examine the brands they used regularly at the time of the interview.

Table 10 describes the 14 tribes from the 1997 first wave of research. At the time this research was presented, we had not considered an overall structure to SA Tribes and no attempt was made to classify the groups in such a way that might shed further meaning, such as the four higher-order groups presented in previous chapters. One could argue that groups (Social Identity Cluster) 1, 2, 5 and 14 represent types of *Rural Survivalists*. Groups 3, 8, 11 and 12 probably sit at the other end of the spectrum as *Urban Elite* or members of an upper *Urban Middle Class*. The balance probably sit somewhere between those extremes.

At the time of this research, we concluded that the two extremes represented people with African or diffuse international identity versus those with European identity. We made the point that, at that particular time, South Africans were likely to be wrestling with identity and battling to find valid comparisons against which to benchmark themselves. We reasoned that the longstanding tendency of South Africans to think of themselves as Europeans and Africans would continue to be influential just three years after the first truly democratic election.

Table 10: *The preliminary 14-cluster SA Tribe solution presented in Montreal*

Social Identity Cluster	Typical characteristics of members
1 (5.4%)	Black, Eastern Cape Province, rural, male, not working, speaks and reads Xhosa, understands English, poverty-stricken, low education, traditional hut, interested in gardening.
2 (6.9%)	Black, rural, female, working, understands Afrikaans, Northern Sotho, Southern Sotho, Tswana, married, poverty-stricken, low education, water to home, interested in women's and children's clothing, DIY and gardening.
3 (7.9%)	White, metropolitan, young, male, not working, English, reads and understands English and Afrikaans, single, high education, all living standard measures present in home but has not bought on credit, savings account, interested in travel and holidays overseas, health and fitness, sport and outdoor activities, stereo and video equipment.
4 (5.4%)	Black, Eastern Cape Province, metropolitan, female, not working, reads Xhosa home language, understands English and Afrikaans, single, low education, water and electricity to home, toilet, refrigerator, TV and stereo, interested in women's and men's clothing, and education.
5 (4.4%)	Black, Limpopo Province, rural, young, male, not working, reads English and Afrikaans, understands Northern Sotho, Southern Sotho and Tswana, single, poverty-stricken, low education, interested in men's clothing, jewellery and fashion accessories, gifts, records, tapes and CDs, education, DIY, travel and holidays within South Africa, health and fitness, and outdoor sporting activities.
6 (6.1%)	Black, KwaZulu-Natal Province, metropolitan, male, not working, understands Zulu, English and Afrikaans, reads Zulu and English, single, low education, matchbox home, electricity and water to home, toilet, refrigerator, TV, stereo, interested in men's clothing, education, health and fitness.
7 (7.4%)	Black, metropolitan, early adult, female, not working, understands Zulu, English, Afrikaans, Northern Sotho, Southern Sotho, Tswana, reads Zulu and English, married, low education, matchbox home, electricity and water to home, toilet, refrigerator, TV, interested in children's and women's clothing, education, home furnishings.
8 (8.4%)	White, metropolitan, early adult, female, working, reads and understands English and Afrikaans, married, high income and education, all living standard measures present in the home, cheque and savings account, ATM card, interested in clothing, jewellery, fashion accessories, cosmetics, toiletries, educational toys, gifts, records, tapes, CDs, sewing, knitting, textiles, education, non-fiction books, children's books, interior decorating, furniture and home furnishings, kitchen and bathroom ware, food and wine, local and international holidays and travel, health and fitness, sports and outdoor activities, gardening, plants and seeds, cats and dogs, insurance, and investment opportunities.
9 (6.7%)	Black, Gauteng Province, metropolitan, early adult, male, working, reads English, Afrikaans, Zulu and Southern Sotho and also understands Xhosa, Northern Sotho and Tswana, married, low education, matchbox home, electricity and water to home, dishwashing liquid, toilet, refrigerator, TV, and stereo, savings account, men's clothing, education and DIY.

Table 10: *(continued)*

Social Identity Cluster	Typical characteristics of members
10 (6.2%)	Black, Gauteng Province, metropolitan, early adult, female, not working, reads English, Afrikaans, Zulu, and Southern Sotho and also understands Xhosa, Northern Sotho and Tswana, single, low education, matchbox home, electricity and water to home, dishwashing liquid, toilet, refrigerator, TV and stereo, interested in clothing, jewellery, fashion accessories, cosmetics, toiletries, educational toys, gifts, records, tapes, CDs, photography, education, children's books, interior decorating, furniture and home furnishings, kitchen and bathroom ware, building and plumbing supplies, DIY, food and wine, local and international holidays and travel, health and fitness, outdoor sporting activities, gardening, plants and seeds, car purchasing, stereo and video equipment, electrical appliances, pensions/retirement, insurance, investment opportunities.
11 (9.4%)	White, metropolitan, early adult, male, working, Afrikaans home language, also reads and understands English, married, high income and education, all living standard measures present in the home, has whole life, endowment, annuity, medical, and short-term insurance policies, cheque and savings accounts, credit and ATM card, DIY, sports and outdoor activities.
12 (10.6%)	White, metropolitan, female, not working, reads English, Afrikaans, married, low education, electricity and water to home, all living standard measures present in the home, savings account, ATM card, interested in gardening.
13 (7.7%)	Coloured, Western Cape Province, female, not working, Afrikaans home language, also understands and reads English, low education, all living standard measures present in the home except a domestic servant.
14 (7.5%)	Black, KwaZulu-Natal Province, rural, female, not working, Zulu home language, also understands English, poverty-stricken, low education, traditional hut, interested in clothing, education and gardening.

Why the clusters differed

The 14 clusters appeared to differ on the basis of race, home language and financial resources. In order to understand better what factors were most influential in determining the group content, a CHAID analysis was run. CHAID is one of a range of related multivariate statistical techniques that produce classification trees, which in turn are used to understand how a group or predictor variables (in this case, the identity variables used to produce the SA Tribes) predict membership in a group (in this case, the individual tribe). CHAID has become a very popular technique in data mining worldwide and was first proposed by Gordon Kass at the University of the Witwatersrand.[5]

Burgess and Harris presented detailed information about the results of the CHAID analysis and I will leave it to readers who wish further details to visit the original paper as published.[6] However, it is important to understand that the variables that most contributed to group identity were living standard measures (hence the title of the article). In fact, the possession of a washing machine emerged as the most influential difference that determined one's group. CHAID analysis allows one to query the analysis and examine possible substitute variables (i.e. to perform a 'what-if' analysis to see what might occur if the washing machine had not been included in the analysis). The substitute variables that emerged as 'next best' predictors included the geyser, motor car and vacuum cleaner/floor polisher. In the present SA Tribes analysis, the geyser emerged as the most important predictor in the determination of group membership.

The results concerning living standard measures bear further discussion. They do not imply that living standard measures are prepotent determinants of human behaviour, or that racial identity is not an important influence. As discussion earlier in this book makes very clear, identity is much more complex and living standard is only one type of observable characteristic. Once the original variable split the data, in all cases, racial identity was the next determinant of importance. Of course, this does not imply genetic causation but rather implies that race is interrelated with the other differences. Again, as the previous chapters have shown, the complexity of identity within situations is something wise people consider carefully.

How identity influenced brand choice

The results of the brand choice analysis of Burgess and Harris are presented in Table 11 beginning on page 80. Some explanation is needed.

We report results for two subsamples of our 3,493 respondents. They are people who have smoked. A total of 1,244 people claimed to have ever smoked one of the listed brands and 843 claimed to be smoking one of them regularly now. Two sets of results are reported: (a) for brands 'ever used' and (b) for brands 'used regularly now'. We examine brand use from both perspectives because it gives us a measure of loyalty over longer and shorter spans of time. We report how well our model identifies (a) people who have smoked a brand and (b) its accuracy in identifying whether a person smoked or did not smoke a brand.

The body of the table reports a series of regression analyses. It is a special type of regression, called *logistic regression*, in which we test how well knowing a respondent's SA Tribes membership 'predicts' he or she having smoked a particular brand of cigarette from our fairly exhaustive list of brands. The Nagelkerke R^2 indicates the strength of the relation between SA Tribe identity and brand choice on a scale of 0 to 1, where 1 is perfectly related and 0 is perfectly unrelated. The results indicate a moderate relationship in most cases, but it is important to note that the strength of the relations varies by brand. This difference can be explained by the strength of the brand image and the strength of its link to identity characteristics. The -2 Log-Likelihood and X^2 (chi-squared) statistics are other measures of fit that will interest some readers. Cluster 14, a group of relatively homogeneous Zulu women living in relative poverty in rural KwaZulu-Natal, was chosen as a reference group for the dummy coding in the logistic regression analysis (i.e. in essence, all other groups are compared to that group in the analysis).

How well does our model predict brand choice? It performs best when predicting the brands people smoked regularly at the time of the interview, correctly identifying more than 80% of the people who smoked Benson & Hedges, Chesterfield, Dunhill or Mills. In fact, it almost identifies every Benson & Hedges smoker.

Our model performs less well in identifying people's smoking behaviour overall. In other words, the model identifies people as smokers of a brand when in fact they are not (i.e. 'false positives') or fails to identify some current smokers. This could be because of a number of factors that we do not know, such as where the brands are advertised or the type and location of outlets where they are sold. This would be especially true in the lower economic strata, where cigarettes are often bought individually in small corner cafés and spaza shops, and buyers must take a cigarette from an open package rather than choose their favourite brand. Thus, people whom the model identified as brand users (whom in truth were not) may have been users if other factors had facilitated the use. On the other hand, it could be that our model of identity has failed to capture identity characteristics that impact more strongly on cigarette consumption.

Modelling is a trial-and-error process that requires some sophistication as regards research design and statistical analysis. Our results are impressive in that we are able to achieve them without benefit of industry experience. Even if we include the two worst 'overall' predicted brands (Dunhill and Mills), knowing someone's SA Tribe improves our ability to predict the brands of cigarettes they use regularly now by 36%.[7]

Industry participant marketing strategies are often a good place to look for cues as to how well any model will predict behaviour. If brands are not differentiated in any way, why would we expect identity or any other variable to aid in predicting behaviour?

What we argue here is that any person who is responsible for understanding how and why people choose and use products and services would

Table 11: *Brand choices of the 14 1997 SA Tribes presented in Montreal*

	Nagelkerke R²	-2 Log-Likelihood for fitted model	X² [a]	Correct Yes	Correct Overall	Clusters more likely to choose this brand [d]	Clusters less likely to choose this brand [d]
Used Regularly Now [b]							
Benson & Hedges	0.373	329	148.47	91.3%	76.4%	3, 8, 11, 12	14
Chesterfield	0.313	339	118.74	83.1%	74.7%	3, 8, 11	14
Dunhill	0.095	231	20.99	82.6%	52.4%	None	14
Mills	0.115	221	24.91	82.1%	55.3%	None	14
Camel	0.260	204	61.36	77.4%	78.8%	None	None
Peter Stuyvesant	0.195	1036	133.11	76.4%	66.1%	None	3, 8, 11, 12
Courtleigh	0.113	453	43.69	72.6%	62.9%	5, 6, 8, 9, 12	14
Consulate	0.138	262	35.40	72.2%	71.3%	7, 9, 10	14
Lexington	0.247	243	66.50	68.4%	77.9%	2	14
Rothmans	0.126	772	69.68	67.9%	65.7%	14	3, 6, 8, 9, 11, 12
Ever Used [c]							
Benson & Hedges	0.267	1173	245.55	84.6%	66.7%	3, 8, 11, 12, 13	14
Chesterfield	0.213	1265	195.57	77.8%	64.0%	3, 8, 11, 12	9, 14
Mills	0.055	1138	41.76	69.0%	54.9%	None	12, 14
Camel	0.280	990	237.14	64.3%	77.9%	3, 8, 11	14
Dunhill	0.105	1233	87.22	64.0%	61.9%	3, 8, 12, 13	14
Lexington	0.099	1233	82.31	63.7%	61.1%	2	9, 14
Peter Stuyvesant	0.161	1329	145.28	63.3%	65.4%	13, 14	2, 8, 11, 12
Courtleigh	0.095	1349	82.66	62.2%	61.5%	5, 6, 13	11, 14
Rothmans	0.075	1574	93.50	58.5%	62.5%	14	3, 6, 8, 9, 11, 12
Consulate	0.109	1234	90.94	58.0%	66.9%	None	1, 2, 3, 8, 11, 12, 14

Note: [a] For difference between null model and fitted model, $p \leq .001$ for all brands, 13 d.f., [b] n=843, [c] n=1244, [d] clusters are grouped by direction of β statistic and are shown only where $p \leq .05$ for the significance test of the Wald statistic with 1 d.f.

find it useful to understand that social identity. We have produced such results in every category that we have analysed during the life of the SA Tribes project – for consumer products, services and even political parties. In some industries, we have achieved 95%+ results in predicting brand users. Some have been less impressive and resulted in predictions that were a bit less accurate than the example above. To some extent, our results are dependent on factors outside our control. When analysing the use of supermarket outlets, for instance, we were at the top of the range because people tend to use many different outlets as and when they are convenient. However, in all cases, understanding identity has enriched our understanding of South African consumers.

Consumer behaviour is an act that involves personal and social choices. Political choices also involve personal and social choices. The following two chapters explore the link between identity and politics. In the next chapter, Professor Bob Mattes explores identity in 11 sub-Saharan African countries, sharing the results of the Afrobarometer project. In Chapter 7 Mari Harris and I explore some selected issues concerning SA Tribes and the political behaviour of the groups.

6: Uniquely African?
What South Africa can learn from the rest of the continent

Social identity is the cause and consequence of many political phenomena.[1] Two of the most important consequences are the stability of political regimes in general and the prospects for consolidating democratic regimes in particular. With this in mind, this chapter summarises a wide range of previously unpublished data from South Africa and ten other African countries, and in the process addresses a few important questions. Aside from the self-interested assertions of political leaders and self-proclaimed group representatives, which social identities do Africans hold first and foremost? Is African identity primarily dominated by racial and ethnic loyalties, or do other identifications play an important role? How has identity been affected during South Africa's transition from Apartheid rule to democratic state? Have primary identifications shifted since 1994? What can South Africans learn from the rest of Africa about identity?

African identities and their link to political attitudes and behaviour have received much attention over the years but there has been very little empirical research from which one might draw conclusions. This chapter responds to that need by reporting the results of research with large, nationally representative datasets in 11 African countries.[2] We consider the results of data collected in South Africa by the Institute for Democracy in South Africa (Idasa) since 1994, and new and original data collected for Afrobarometer – a large-scale cross-national research project that measures citizens' attitudes toward democracy, markets and civil society. Afrobarometer is organised as an international collaborative network run by three core partners: the Institute for Democracy in South Africa, the Centre for Democratic Development in Ghana (CDD-Ghana), and Michigan State University. National research institutions affiliated with the Afrobarometer project conducted the fieldwork. We are grateful for research funding from the National Science Foundation, United States Agency for International Development, Swedish International Development Agency and the Danish Trust Fund at the World Bank.

The data reviewed in this chapter comes from systematic surveys of random stratified probability samples in 11 African states, seven in southern

Africa (Botswana, Lesotho, Malawi, Namibia, South Africa, Zambia and Zimbabwe), two in east Africa (Tanzania and Uganda) and two in west Africa (Mali and Nigeria), all conducted between July 1999 and September 2001. A caveat is in order regarding our ability to generalise the results presented here to wider African populations. Each country sample was drawn independently and randomly, representing voting age populations.[3] The 11 countries are largely English-speaking and all have recently undergone political transitions to multi-party systems (with the exception of Uganda) and are not fully representative of sub-Saharan Africa. We cannot infer the findings of this paper to francophone Africa, to the continent's remaining authoritarian regimes or to states imploding through civil war. Though we may use the shorthand term 'Africans' often, we have a more limited populace in mind.

Why is social identity important in politics?

When they drew new and highly artificial political boundaries during Europe's 'scramble for Africa', colonial cartographers divided and re-combined existing identity groups into new and highly diverse communities. Considerable scholarship has focused on the dangers of such social diversity and the possibilities of transforming or transcending it. Some scholars have presumed that the pre-existing identities were so strong and relatively fixed as to be primordial in nature. Clearly, if pre-existing identities were so powerful, these identities would pose a significant obstacle to post-independence attempts to develop new national identities.[4] People would identify first and foremost with their primary social or solidity group and only secondarily, if at all, with the post-independence national political entity.[5] Indeed, scholars who have attributed much importance to pre-existing identities have tended to see primary group identity and post-independence national identity to be in tension with one another, if not mutually exclusive. To the extent that both identities coexisted, they have argued that the more citizens identified with some sub-national solidity group, the less they would identify with the overarching national political community.[6] If one carries such thinking to its logical conclusion, one is confronted with the obvious implication that the consequent lack of national identity would rob newly independent states of the necessary 'political glue'. Every element of political conflict is turned into a zero-sum group-based game that threatens the very stability of the new polity.

In addition to the undesirable implications for political stability, diverse social identities are also thought to limit the prospects for the consolidation of political systems that incorporate a substantial democratic component.[7] This is because democracy presumes at least some prior agreement on the identity of the nation (i.e. who is included in 'the people') that is to govern itself democratically. While democracy allows people to govern their own affairs, it cannot tell us which people should be included or excluded from the process of ruling with a given political unit. To paraphrase Ernst Gellner, democracy cannot tell us 'who chooses the choosers?'[8]

Sharing many of these basic presumptions, Africa's post-independence leaders tended to see the ethnic, religious and racial diversity contained within their new states as a threat to their very stability (and ironically, often used this as an excuse to curtail multi-party competition). Many embarked upon projects of aggressive 'nation-building' to inculcate psychological affinities between newly defined citizens and the political territories in which they lived, and to break down older and more traditional identifications. Policy makers have used a wide range of policies to accomplish such objectives – such as imposing national languages, creating new national symbols and holidays, or fostering new values through school curriculum and state media. Yet, many scholars have warned repeatedly of the near impossibility of building national identity, generally arguing that such attempts amount to no more than 'Jacobinist' impositions of the values, symbols and culture of the politically dominant group on the rest of society.[9] South Africa continues to witness such debates.[10]

Evidence from South Africa

Apartheid social engineering manipulated racial and ethnic identities. Many scholars predicted that Apartheid identities would quickly be jettisoned with the advent of democracy.[11] However, it seems clear that many South Africans may not dismiss the consequences of 40 years of social engineering and the previous history of racial separation so easily. Apartheid's legacy may very well leave a heavy imprint on social identities that will constrain or at least impact on the future development of democracy.[12]

In this section, we examine evidence about the type and extent of social identities in South Africa, as well as the salience with which they are held. This South African data was not collected as part of the SA Tribes project, but rather as part of on-going research at Idasa. In fact, Professor Burgess and I were unaware of one another's research on identity until after this data had been collected.

The Idasa research did not set out to construct social identity groups from the complex mix of variables associated with identity, such as SA Tribes has done. Our goal was to ascertain perceived primary social identifications and explore some very basic and important political questions related to identity. We wondered to what extent South Africans still identified with Apartheid social identities some six years into their new non-racial democracy. Were social identities widely diverse or consensual? How had identities changed, if at all, since 1994? Finally, did identity perceptions detract or contribute towards a widespread acceptance of the political entity called South Africa, an acceptance of one's place in South Africa, and pride in South African citizenship?

Focusing on primary social identifications,[13] we asked respondents to tell us the social group to which they belonged first and foremost – in addition to being South African (the actual wording can be found in the note to Table 12). We then asked a set of questions designed to assess the extent to which people perceived these identities as meaningful in their lives.

The results suggest that substantial proportions of South Africans still primarily identify themselves in terms of Apartheid-type categories six years into their new democracy. In the third quarter of 2000, 20% chose a group that expressed an explicit Apartheid racial identity: 12% said black, 5% Coloured, 3% Indian, 2% white, and another 1% simply answered that they thought of themselves in terms of race. Another 9% answered African, which in the South African context is generally used to connote black – and another 1% called themselves black African.

So how did people who did not choose an Apartheid racial identity as their primary identification describe their group? Twenty percent chose a linguistic or ethnic identity. Seven percent said Zulu, 5% Xhosa, 2% Setswana or Tswana, and 1% each chose Afrikaner, Sesotho or Sotho, Swazi, Boer or English. Sixteen percent chose a religious category, with 13% thinking of themselves primarily as Christian, 2% as a religious person and 1% each as Muslim and Catholic.

We wondered how these identification patterns have changed over time. To answer this question, we review previous Idasa surveys beginning immediately after the country's first open democratic election. While the 1994 and 1995 questions differ in important ways from the questions used in 1997 and 2000[14] (see endnote), it does appear that there has been a significant drop in the proportions holding racially based social identities, and marked increases in those adopting religious, class or occupational identities. Yet, as important as these trends may be, racial and ethnic loyalties are still the most prevalent sources for identity in South Africa.

But are these identities mere labels or are they important to peoples' lives? Since 1997, Idasa has presented respondents with six statements about their

Table 12: *Primary identifications, South Africa 2000*

Primary identification	Total (%)	Asian (%)	Black (%)	Coloured (%)	White (%)
Christian	13	4	13	18	8
Black	12	1	17	0	1
African	9	0	13	1	<1
Zulu	7	0	10	0	0
Middle Class	7	1	2	7	32
Ordinary person	6	4	7	7	2
Xhosa	5	0	7	0	0
Coloured	5	0	0	46	0
Working Class	4	4	2	7	14
Indian	3	69	0	0	0
Setswana/Tswana	2	0	3	0	0
White	2	0	0	0	13
Religious	2	0	1	2	3
Muslim	1	8	0	4	<1
Catholic	1	0	1	1	0
Black African	1	0	1	0	<1
In terms of race	1	0	1	0	<1
Afrikaner	1	0	0	0	4
Sesotho	1	0	1	0	0
Boer	1	0	<1	0	3
English	1	0	<1	0	1
Swazi	1	0	1	0	0
Poor	1	0	1	2	1
Worker	1	0	1	1	<1
Student	1	0	1	0	1
Political party member	1	0	1	0	3
Did not differentiate self	<1	0	0	1	2
Other	7	0	0	0	0
Nothing	2	0	2	2	2
Refused	<1	0	0	0	<1

Note: Reported are percentages of each column. The following question was asked: 'We have spoken to many South Africans and they have all described themselves in different ways. Some people describe themselves in terms of their language, religion, race, and others describe themselves in economic terms, such as working class, middle class, or a farmer. Besides being South African, which specific group do you feel you belong to first and foremost?' (Source: Afrobarometer, 2000)

Table 13: *Primary identifications, South Africa 1994–2000*

	1994	1995	1997	2000		1994	1995	1997	2000
Religion					**Race**				
Christian	2	1	6	13	Black	14	16	16	12
Religious	1	1	1	2	Coloured	5	4	5	5
Muslim	<1	<1	1	1	White	14	5	3	2
Catholic	0	0	1	1	Black African	0	0	0	1
Other Religions	<1	<1	4	<1	In terms of race	0	0	0	1
Language/Tribe					**Continental**				
Zulu	7	8	12	7	African	2	4	5	9
Xhosa	1	2	6	5	Asian	0	<1	2	<1
Indian	1	2	2	3	**Personal**				
Setswana/Tswana	1	1	4	2	Ordinary person	1	1	<1	6
Afrikaner/Afrikaans	4	5	4	1	Other	1	1	2	7
Sesotho	1	1	4	1	Nothing	1	3	<1	2
Boer	<1	<1	<1	1	Don't differentiate self	0	0	0	<1
English	2	4	1	1	Refused	0	0	<1	<1
Swazi	2	<1	3	1	**Occupation**				
Tsonga/Shangaan	2	1	2	0	Occupation	0	<1	<1	<1
Ndebele	0	0	1	0	Student	0	0	<1	1
Sepedi	2	2	5	<1	**Region**				
Venda	1	1	1	<1	Region	0	4	0	0
Class					**Party Affiliation**				
Middle Class	0	<1	4	7	In terms of				
Working Class	<1	<1	2	4	political party	0	0	<1	1
Poor	0	0	<1	1	South African	13	22	*	
Worker	0	0	<1	1					

Note: Reported are percentages of each column.[14]
*Four percent still offered this response in 1997 despite the question wording.

Table 14: *Primary identifications by category, South Africa 1994–2000*

	1994	1995	1997	2000
Race	33	24	24	22
Language	24	27	45	20
Religion	4	3	13	16
Class/Occupation	<1	1	7	14
Partisan	0	0	<1	1
Continental	2	4	7	9
Regional	0	4	<1	0
Nothing/Won't Differentiate/Refuse	1	3	<1	3

Note: Reported are percentages of each column (i.e. by year).

identity and asked them to agree or disagree with each. Subsequent analysis, however, has suggested that these six items actually tap two different, though related, aspects of group identity. The first three items measure one's personal group identity (see Table 15). This dimension measures the salience of in-group identification for each respondent.

The second set of statements taps a different and related dimension that appears to be produced by the in-group favouritism effect that was discussed in detail in Chapter 2 of this book. We have called this dimension *group chauvinism* (see Table 16). Group chauvinism refers to the respondents' perceptions of in-group superiority and distinctiveness.

As regards the respondents' *strength of personal group identity*, the results suggest that many South Africans feel strong attachment to group identity. For instance, in 2000, 92% of South Africans said that being a member of

Table 15: *Strength of personal group identity, South Africa 1997–2000*

	June/July 1997	July/Aug 2000
It makes you feel proud to be a _____ .	83	92
Being _____ is a very important part of how you see yourself.	89	90
You would want your children to think of themselves as _____ .	86	84

Note: Reported are percentages of total respondents in each survey period that selected 'strongly agree' or 'agree'. The group selected by each respondent was inserted in the blank space for each question.

Table 16: *Sense of group chauvinism, South Africa 1997–2000*

	June/July 1997	July/Aug 2000
You feel much closer to _____s than other South Africans.	78	73
Of all the groups in South Africa, _____s are the best.	56	64
_____ people are very different from other South Africans.	49	49

Note: Reported are percentages of total respondents in each survey period that selected 'strongly agree' or 'agree'. The group selected by each respondent was inserted in the blank space for each question.

their identity group made them feel proud, 90% agreed that being a member of that group was a very important part of one's self-perception. Eighty-four percent said that they would want their children to think of themselves in these terms. A comparison of each of these responses in 2000 with 1997 reveals no clear trends.

As noted earlier, the second set of items measures a sense of group chauvinism within the group. In 2000, three-quarters (73%) of South Africans said that they felt much closer to members of their identity group than to other South Africans. Sixty-four percent felt that their group was the best of all the groups in South Africa and 49% felt that members of their group were very different from other South Africans.

Clearly, when comparing the lower endorsement by respondents of the items in Table 16 to their endorsements of the items in Table 15, these results imply that many South Africans who hold strong group loyalties can hold them in such a way that is not necessarily chauvinistic or exclusive. As was the case with the items in Table 15, a comparison of Table 16 across the two time periods reveals no clear trends of either increasing or decreasing levels of group chauvinism.

If South Africans exhibit apparently strong attachments to their sub-national group identities, does this detract from the creation of a widely shared sense of national identity? The results presented in Table 17 suggest that the answer is emphatically 'no'. South Africans exhibit extremely high levels of national identity. In 2000, 90% said it made them proud to be called South African, 89% agreed that being South African is an important part of how they see themselves; the same proportion said that they would want their children to think of themselves as South African.

When this data is viewed over time and isolated by race, we see that levels of national identity among black South Africans have remained

Table 17: *Strength of national identity, South Africa 1995–2000*

	1995	1997	Nov 1998	July 2000
It makes you proud to be called a South African.	91	94	91	90
Being South African is an important part of how you see yourself.	N/A	91	90	89
You would want your children to think of themselves as South African.	N/A	N/A	92	89

Note: Reported are percentages of total respondents in each survey period that selected 'strongly agree' or 'agree'.

constant since 1995 but there have been substantial declines among Asian, Coloured and white respondents.

While people seem to be in agreement about their personal commitment and loyalty to South Africa, to what extent do they hold an inclusive, or what might be called 'rainbow', definition of that citizenship? There is widespread endorsement (91%) of the statement that all naturally born South Africans should receive equal treatment regardless of their group identity. Most people

Table 18: *Sense of national identity, South Africa 1995–2000*

	1995	1997	1998	2000
Proud to be called South African citizen				
Asian	92	89	84	84
Black	93	95	95	94
Coloured	94	92	95	87
White	87	85	73	75
Being South African is an important part of how I see myself				
Asian	N/A	97	84	78
Black	N/A	91	93	91
Coloured	N/A	93	94	89
White	N/A	85	73	76
I want my children to think of themselves as South Africans				
Asian	N/A	N/A	89	85
Black	N/A	N/A	94	92
Coloured	N/A	N/A	96	93
White	N/A	N/A	77	75

Note: Reported are percentages of total respondents in each survey period that selected 'strongly agree' or 'agree'.

Table 19: *Inclusiveness of national identity, South Africa 1997–2000*

	1997	1998	2000
All people who were born in this country, regardless of what group they belong to, should be treated as equal citizens of South Africa.	N/A	N/A	91
People should realise we are South Africans first and stop thinking of themselves as Afrikaner, Zulu or whatever.	82	89	N/A
It is desirable to create one united South African nation out of all the different groups who live in this country.	83	86	85
It is possible to create one united South African nation out of all the different groups who live in this country.	67	75	77

Note: Reported are percentages of total respondents in each survey period that selected 'strongly agree' or 'agree'.

(85%) also endorse the statement that it is desirable to build one united South Africa out of all the groups living in the country. A large but smaller majority (77%) felt it was possible to create a united South African nation.

Closer examination of respondents' opinions, within racial categories and over time (see Table 20 on page 92), reveals that whites are generally less likely than other South Africans to agree that people should stop thinking of themselves in group terms, less likely to support equal treatment for all regardless of group of origin, and less likely to feel that building one united nation was desirable or possible. Nevertheless, it is important to consider these findings in context. First, it should be noted that the only item in Table 20 that is not endorsed by a majority of whites concerns their belief in the possibility of creating a united South African nation from the different groups. That is to say, they endorse the latent notion of nation-building that underlies the items but appear to have difficulty accepting that the ideal can be reached in a practical world. Second, when compared to their position in 1997, white South Africans have become more supportive of a common nation-building project and more likely to believe it can be done.

Conclusions from South Africa

This brief review of South African political attitudes allows us to draw a few important generalisations. First, South Africans have achieved the invaluable prerequisite of political stability and democratic consolidation: that is, they have reached a near consensual agreement that the legally defined political community is the appropriate one, that they are indeed members of that com-

Table 20: *Perceptions of national identity, South Africa 1997–2001*

	1997	1998	2000
People should think of themselves as South Africans first			
Asian	79	92	N/A
Black	83	92	N/A
Coloured	90	96	N/A
White	68	74	N/A
Equal treatment regardless of group identity			
Asian	N/A	N/A	96
Black	N/A	N/A	90
Coloured	N/A	N/A	98
White	N/A	N/A	79
Desirable to create one united South African nation out of all groups			
Asian	88	91	95
Black	86	89	88
Coloured	94	91	95
White	58	66	64
Possible to create one united South African nation			
Asian	72	69	79
Black	72	82	82
Coloured	70	78	82
White	32	41	44

Note: Reported are percentages of total respondents in each survey period who selected 'strongly agree' or 'agree'.

munity, and that they are proud of that membership. This might seem obvious now, but key political analysts and commentators for years warned that there would be insufficient 'glue' to hold the country together under a democratic dispensation.[15] Second, race and ethnicity remain important facets of social identity that people feel first and foremost. However, this tendency appears to be decreasing and other facets of social identity – such as religious, class or occupational – appear to be assuming primary importance for many South Africans. Third, high levels of national identity and loyalty can coexist with equally high levels of identification with sub-national social identity groups. In other words, to the extent that there has been a nation-building project since 1994, it has not transformed group identities into national identity (or transferred loyalty from one to the other). Rather, it has created the awareness and endorsement of a transcendent national identity that overarches but coexists with other facets of social identity.

Evidence from the rest of Africa

We now turn to evidence from the Afrobarometer research project to help us understand our South African findings in the larger regional context. The comparison allows us to see important differences and parallels between South Africa and other African countries, which in each instance may run counter to what we might have expected. As with South Africa, African identity generally has been conceptualised as a primary identification with pre-modern and virtually primordial ethnic or tribal ties. Scholars often distinguish African politics on the very fact that 'modern' identities such as those based on class or occupational categories have yet to develop.

Table 21 presents results to the question on the facet of social identity felt first and foremost by respondents in 11 African countries, including South Africa. In five countries, the most common primary identification was ethnic, linguistic or tribal: Nigeria (48%), Namibia (45%), Mali (39%,) Malawi (38%) and South Africa (22%). Yet, religion also emerged as an important primary identification in Zambia (35%), Lesotho (27%), Malawi (26%), Mali (23%), Nigeria (21%) and South Africa (18%). It is not surprising that racial identifications emerge as primary identity facets that are held by significant proportions in the three former settler colonies: South Africa (20%), Namibia (12%) and Zimbabwe (12%).

But in contrast to the commonly advanced viewpoint that tribal and ethnic identifications dominate Africans' perceptions of themselves, occupational and class identities were the most frequent primary identifications in Tanzania (80%), Uganda (68%), Lesotho (60%), Zambia (48%) and Zimbabwe (38%). Even if one takes out occupational categories that could reflect more traditional identifications such as 'farmer' or 'fisherman', explicitly class-based primary identifications are widely held in Lesotho (29%), Zambia (23%) and Zimbabwe (19%). It is noteworthy that class-based identifications are relatively rare in South Africa, given that it is the most industrialised country on the continent with a thriving trade union movement. Thus, while communal identities still feature prominently, the surprising frequency with which Africans call on economic or class identities challenges many assumptions about the supposed 'primordialism' of identity in African politics.

It may also surprise some that South Africans' high levels of group identity are not atypical. Most countries resemble South Africa in terms of very

Table 21: *Primary identifications in 11 Afrobarometer countries*

Primary identification	Botswana	Lesotho	Malawi	Mali	Namibia	Nigeria
Continental	<1	<1	1	0	<1	0
Linguistic/ethnic/tribal	28	2	38	39	46	48
Race	3	<1	1	0	12	0
Region	17	0	1	<1	0	0
Religious	5	27	26	23	6	21
Occupation	8	31	22	7	20	18
Class	2	29	5	16	16	10
Gender	0	0	0	4	<1	0
Personal	<1	4	<1	4	0	2
Party affiliation	3	<1	<1	0	<1	0
Other	<1	1	<1	6	<1	0
Won't differentiate	32	1	<1	<1	<1	0
Don't know/nothing	2	4	6	0	0	0

Note: Reported are percentages of total respondents in each country. Respondents were asked the following question, customised to their country: 'We have spoken to many [insert nationality] and they have all described themselves in different ways. Some people describe themselves in terms of their language, religion, race, and others describe themselves in economic terms, such as working class, middle class or farmer. Besides being [insert nationality], which specific group do you feel you belong to first and foremost?'

strong attachments to group identities. Only Zimbabweans and the Basotho stand out by according significantly lower levels of salience to their identities. South Africans also fail to corner the market with regard to group chauvinism; Nigerians are far more likely to see their group identities in chauvinist terms (Table 22).

The high levels of national identity reported by South Africans are mirrored in other regional countries (Table 22). In eight of the nine countries where these questions were asked, majorities ranging from 89% to 97% stated that they were proud to be called citizens of their country and that they wanted their children to think of themselves as citizens of the country. In Zimbabwe, the proportion agreeing with these statements dropped to 84% and 78% respectively. Most of these countries also resemble South Africa with regard to respondents' willingness to extend equal citizenship status to members of other groups, and the desire to create one united nation out of all people living in the country. Lesotho was the exception with only 70% in agreement with these statements.

Primary identification	South Africa	Tanzania	Uganda	Zambia	Zimbabwe
Continental	9	0	0	<1	1
Linguistic/ethnic/tribal	22	3	12	8	35
Race	20	<1	0	5	12
Region	<1	<1	1	0	0
Religious	18	4	8	35	8
Occupation	2	77	63	25	19
Class	14	3	5	23	18
Gender	<1	8	6	0	0
Personal	3	<1	2	<1	0
Party affiliation	1	<1	0	0	0
Other	8	4	1	<1	0
Won't differentiate	<1	<1	2	1	2
Don't know/nothing	2	0	1	2	4

A final comment seems appropriate with regard to these indicators of national identity. Given the broad levels of agreement, one is tempted to disregard them as 'motherhood' questions that tap attitudes so unobjectionable as to be meaningless. It could also be argued that the questions encourage respondents to produce a 'politically correct' answer that they think is socially desirable, although we did not measure social desirability in the present research.[16] In lieu of such evidence, the past few decades of scholarship on African politics gives us reason to feel very confident about our results. Consider that, even if people were offering what they feel is a socially desirable response, it is noteworthy that they think that exhibiting a high degree of national identity is so desirable. Also, although we have aggregated the 'agree' and 'strongly agree' responses in these tables to simplify the presentation of our results to a wider audience and in book form, there are important variations in the proportions who choose each response and identify with the national political community at lukewarm rather than more intense levels. Research has shown that even though

Table 22: *Comparing South Africa to other African countries*

	Botswana	Lesotho	Malawi	Mali	Namibia	Nigeria
You feel proud to be _____.	94	64	94	98	90	97
You would want your children to think of themselves as _____.	88	59	89	—	82	90
Of all the groups in this country, _____ people are the best.	50	56	46	—	62	80
You feel much stronger ties to _____s than to other _____s.	64	63	53	—	69	88
It makes you proud to be called a _____.	95	95	97	95		
You would want your children to think of themselves as _____.	95	94	97	93		
All people who were born in this country, regardless of what group they belong to, should be treated as equal citizens of _____.	88	72	92	87		
It is desirable to create one united _____ nation out of all the different groups who live in this country.	85	71	94	82		

Note: Reported are percentages of total respondents in each survey period who selected 'strongly agree' or 'agree'.

overall levels of national identity are widespread, the degree to which people possess more intense versus more lukewarm levels of national identity is an important predictor of South Africans' willingness to serve in the country's military forces, the emigration potential of skilled white South Africans, and Africans' support for a democratic regime.[17]

African conclusions

Respected scholar of African politics David Welsh observed that to his knowledge:

> '… in no single attested case since the proliferation of independent, ex-colonial states began after 1945, has "nation building", as a conscious attempt to detach people's loyalties from sub-national entities and focus them on a putative "nation", succeeded.'[18]

	South Africa	Tanzania	Uganda	Zambia	Zimbabwe
You feel proud to be _____.	92	93	—	87	76
You would want your children to think of themselves as _____.	84	—	—	78	71
Of all the groups in this country, _____ people are the best.	64	—	—	55	50
You feel much stronger ties to _____s than to other _____s.	73	—	—	54	67
It makes you proud to be called a _____.	90			95	84
You would want your children to think of themselves as _____.	89			95	78
All people who were born in this country, regardless of what group they belong to, should be treated as equal citizens of _____.	91			87	88
It is desirable to create one united _____ nation out of all the different groups who live in this country.	85			90	92

While he is certainly correct about loyalties and sub-national entities, Welsh (and many others) failed to anticipate that this was not a necessary part of creating new nations. While far from complete, this evidence suggests that the process of post-independence nation-building has created coherent political communities with high levels of national identity in at least 11 African countries. As with South Africa, it appears that this national identity is a transcendent one – in that it bridges but coexists with high levels of group identity. And while we have no prior data for comparison, there is evidence that in at least some countries, political engineering and modernisation have helped transform the nature of social identity away from tribe and language toward economic function and class.

Thus, we see the incredible complexity of primary social identifications in Africa and the diversity that can be witnessed on the continent. In the next chapter, Steve Burgess and Mari Harris delve further into the political implications of social identity by examining the political choices and voting intentions of the 16 SA Tribes.

7: One South African, one vote
Is democracy working and do we care?

As the previous chapter shows, race and ethnicity may be important influences on social identities in some African countries, but other characteristics often dominate identifications elsewhere in the continent. The most influential identifications may be economic, social or occupational, as Professor Mattes points out and as discussed in earlier chapters.

Many identity characteristics have been linked to political behaviour. This is not surprising. After all, political attitudes and behaviour are intrinsically social perceptions and acts. If the major premise of SA Tribes – that identity is a major influence on social attitudes and behaviours – is correct, then we should expect the 16 tribes to differ in their political views and voting preferences. And they do. In fact, on a series of political questions that we have surveyed over the years, the probability that they do not differ in their political attitudes and intended voting choices has been less than 1 in 1,000 in every comparison we have analysed.

Thinking of people as members of identity groups offers the same advantages to political scientists that it does to consumer researchers. Instead of thinking of voters in terms of their Apartheid racial identities (which seems to be the case in so much of the popular discussion of voters and their preferences), one can conceptualise a dynamic set of voters who are likely to be interested in solving rather different problems in their lives.

In this chapter, we examine a selection of political attitudes and political party preferences of the 16 tribes. We begin by examining how the respondents reacted when asked how they thought the South African government was *controlling inflation*. Our focus then shifts to a larger economic question: how well they thought the government was *managing the economy*. The government has had important successes in addressing two primary goals for reconstruction: *building houses for the homeless* and *providing basic health care services* to the needy. We examine these issues and then move on to the potentially more contentious issue of *fighting corruption in government*. These questions are prime delivery areas by which voters are evaluating the government. They give us an exciting opportunity to determine whether knowing someone's SA Tribe helps us understand their views on political issues.

We close the chapter by examining the voting intentions of all the groups. Do they perceive life to be getting better or worse? We report their voting intentions at the time, if an election had been held the next day. We help explain the voting preferences by examining the respondents' views of life compared to a year ago and their expectations of life in one year's time.

Controlling inflation

One of the South African government's economic successes has been its success in controlling inflation, which since 1994 has reached its lowest levels in a generation. Inflation is defined as a relatively sustained period of increasing consumer prices or as steadily decreasing purchasing power. It means people can buy less with their money and it occurs when available currency and credit outrun available goods and services.

Inflation is not a simple concept to understand. When Teddy Langschmidt presented his *Third Alternative Education Crisis Alliance* results in the early 1990s, he noted that one-third of the black South Africans over the age of 35 who were surveyed had never participated in a mathematics course of any kind. Children in almost two-thirds of black homes did not have their own bed to sleep in or place to study. In Chapter 4, we noted that one in seven *Rural Survivalists* has never attended school and four in ten have not completed primary school.

It is not hard to hypothesise about how different access to economic and educational resources might affect the political attitudes of the respondents. Few *Rural Survivalists* have liquid assets of any kind that might decline in value. They live for today. There is no money to save. Everything goes into survival and the future value of anything is of little consequence or concern. Life takes place from day-to-day and moment-to-moment.

Emerging Consumers, on the other hand, have begun to benefit from the government's attempts to increase the quality of life for ordinary South Africans, perhaps more than any other tribe. Although many *Emerging Consumers* live in very poor circumstances and they have been deprived access to an education, we can assume that the economic future looks brighter to them than it does to other groups, especially those that are dominated by youth. There is an exception. We can expect *Cape Coloured Emerging* to see less relative improvement in the future than other *Emerging Consumers* (perhaps because, in general, they were relatively better off in the past – although also disadvantaged).[1]

We can expect *Emerging Consumers* and the *Urban Elite* to have very different perceptions of inflation. They are employed and have acquired some

Table 23: *Controlling inflation*

Controlling inflation: how well would you say the government is handling this?

Group	Very well %	Fairly well %	Not very well %	Not at all well %	Don't know %	Refused %
Agrarian Lifestyles	6.9	34.9	29.1	17.2	11.8	
Border Survivalists	7.1	44.6	34.1	5.6	8.5	
Highveld Survivalists	11.4	39.0	33.3	11.1	5.2	
KZN Survivalists	2.3	27.8	30.8	35.0	4.2	
Free State Emerging	20.5	55.7	21.9	1.9		
Matchbox Suburban Youth	17.6	37.1	33.9	9.1	2.3	
Gauteng Township Youth	11.4	44.8	30.7	8.5	4.5	0.1
Cape Coloured Emerging	2.7	16.4	55.0	19.4	6.6	
Prime Skills	11.3	45.2	33.5	9.4	0.7	
East Coast Settlers	1.5	16.9	46.9	32.7	1.5	0.5
The Believers	3.4	25.4	39.8	30.1	0.8	0.5
Suburban Bliss	5.4	28.7	40.2	22.2	2.8	0.7
Suburban Challenge	6.7	29.2	35.1	29.1		
Earth Mothers	4.4	37.7	36.3	20.8	0.8	
Family Focus	5.7	21.6	35.2	34.7	0.7	2.1
Achievers	14.7	37.6	24.5	22.8	0.5	
National Average	9.2	36.5	33.6	16.1	4.5	0.1

assets. Survival is not always the central concern of every waking moment; they are making purchase and consumption choices that often require them to plan for large future purchases or investments.

We might intuitively expect evaluations of the government's handling of inflation to rise with education and access to formal news media, as reports have been very favourable for some time. However, it is not so simple. On the one hand, the more educated and informed people are, the more we can expect them to realise that the government is doing a pretty good job. On the other hand, the greater their interest in the future value of the currency – whether that be because they are of retirement age or simply wealthy – then we can expect them to be more concerned that the inflation rate generally remains above that of South Africa's more industrialised trading partners. Thus we can expect evaluations to rise with education and access to formal financial news media, and then to fall as assets rise to a point that people feel inflation may erode the investments they expect to rely on in the future. This suggests a curvilinear relationship with evaluations peaking in the 'middle'.

The results appear in Table 23. The *Emerging Consumers*, with the expected exception of the *Cape Coloured Emerging*, feel the government is doing the best job. *Achievers* are also more positive than the national average, perhaps feeling they are savvy enough to protect themselves.

Managing the economy

We can expect the perception of the government's handling of the economy – a more general economic attitude – to be similar to the way its handling of inflation is regarded. From the perspective of 'what's in it for me?' both concepts concern money in the consumer's pockets, at least to some extent, and both require one to have a relatively sophisticated understanding of the inner workings of an economy in order to form an informed opinion.

Table 24: *Managing the economy*

Managing the economy: how well would you say the government is handling this?

Group	Very well %	Fairly well %	Not very well %	Not at all well %	Don't know %	Refused %
Agrarian Lifestyles	8.1	36.4	29.7	14.8	10.9	
Border Survivalists	6.3	51.4	27.7	1.0	13.7	
Highveld Survivalists	20.8	38.2	25.9	10.8	4.2	
KZN Survivalists	3.6	33.1	34.3	22.1	6.9	
Free State Emerging	25.3	46.8	22.7	3.9	1.3	
Matchbox Suburban Youth	25.5	44.0	22.6	6.3	1.6	0.1
Gauteng Township Youth	17.4	46.5	28.3	5.7	2.2	
Cape Coloured Emerging	5.2	26.8	40.6	19.9	7.4	
Prime Skills	16.8	46.8	28.5	7.2	0.7	
East Coast Settlers	0.8	25.8	34.5	37.5	0.8	
The Believers	1.8	25.1	38.7	32.3	1.5	
Suburban Bliss	3.3	36.3	38.3	19.0	2.5	
Suburban Challenge	1.6	34.6	35.6	28.2		
Earth Mothers	2.7	35.0	30.9	28.2	3.2	
Family Focus	4.4	13.8	38.1	41.6		2.1
Achievers	2.6	49.1	22.4	25.4	0.5	
National Average	12.1	39.1	29.6	14.3	4.7	0.1

The results show a similar pattern, with the exception that the views are generally more favourable among the *Rural Survivalists* and *Emerging Consumers* and less favourable elsewhere (Table 24).

Building houses for the poor

In the period since the Government of National Unity came into power in 1994, over one million homes have been built for the poor. Figure 6 shows progress in housing construction through 2000. Minister Trevor Manuel gave attendees at the 2000 University of Cape Town Graduate School of Business Annual Dinner a real insight by comparing South Africa's progress to other countries – theirs is a real *Guinness Book of World Records* performance. In fact, building development to date dwarfs that of the first 25 years of government-subsidised private housing construction achieved by the previous record-holder, Singapore, by almost a factor of two – in less than one-third of the time.

Figure 6: *Houses started or completed 1994–2000, by province*
(Source: Ministry of Housing)

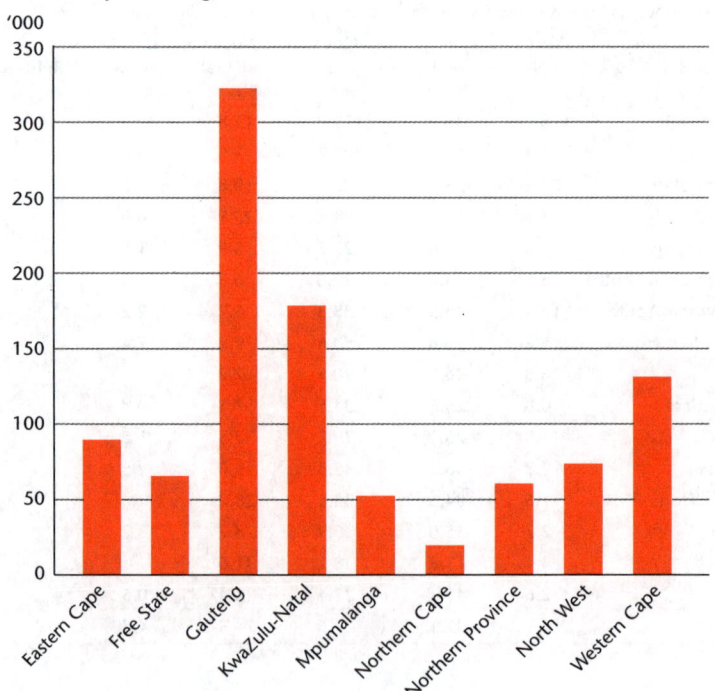

Table 25: *Building houses for the poor*

Building houses for the poor: how well would you say the government is handling this?

Group	Very well %	Fairly well %	Not very well %	Not at all well %	Don't know %	Refused %
Agrarian Lifestyles	21.2	41.6	17.2	18.6	1.4	
Border Survivalists	15.4	57.1	25.0	2.5		
Highveld Survivalists	22.6	32.7	25.5	19.2		
KZN Survivalists	16.6	40.9	16.2	26.2		
Free State Emerging	48.7	32.6	18.7			
Matchbox Suburban Youth	30.6	44.2	14.2	11.1		
Gauteng Township Youth	31.4	50.9	13.8	3.7	0.1	0.1
Cape Coloured Emerging	8.2	36.8	45.5	8.9	0.5	
Prime Skills	30.6	46.8	11.3	10.5	0.7	
East Coast Settlers	5.8	44.1	26.1	23.5		0.5
The Believers	8.6	43.6	32.7	14.1	0.5	0.5
Suburban Bliss	16.6	48.4	25.5	8.7	0.2	0.7
Suburban Challenge	12.5	43.9	34.0	9.6		
Earth Mothers	4.8	52.1	32.6	10.5		
Family Focus	7.8	36.2	31.2	21.8	0.9	2.1
Achievers	7.0	59.8	19.2	13.6	0.5	
National Average	21.5	43.4	21.7	13.0	0.3	0.1%

Can one expect such progress to be universally recognised by South Africans as excellent? How can we expect the respondents to rate their government's performance?

Table 25 shows a pattern that we might expect. *Rural survivalists* have not really benefited from the housing programme and they are the most desperately in need. Nonetheless, many are on waiting lists and most will know of someone who has benefited. We can expect them to be less enthusiastic than the national average but not substantially so. The *Emerging Consumers*, who have benefited most, can be expected to be the most approving in their evaluations – with the exception of the *Cape Coloured Emerging* community for the same reason previously noted. We can expect the managerial class of South Africans, the *Urban Elite*, to be most negative because of their knowledge of the teething problems that have received so much press attention and because of their proximity to the more established, professional management practices in the private sector.

Providing basic health services

The government's performance in this area has received much attention. There has been controversy over the HIV/AIDS position of the government, especially policy issues such as the provision of nevirapine to pregnant mothers. Newspapers, talk radio stations and many other media outlets have focused on health delivery issues daily for years now.

We would expect people's responses to this question to be determined by the meaning they attach to the words 'basic health services'. To the *Urban Elite*, basic health services may include the extensive range of services one expects to be available in the world's most industrialised regions. CAT scanners, laser surgery, arthroscopic procedures, advanced non-invasive diagnostic procedures. Such services may seem far less important to *Rural Survivalists* or *Emerging Consumers*. They still witness unacceptably high levels of infant mortality, unsafe drinking water, malnutrition and lack of access to primary health care.

Primary health care was really the focus of the question, but we can expect the more holistic set of perceptual differences as to the meaning of 'basic health services' to affect the responses to the question. Thus, we expect evaluations that are more favourable from the *Rural Survivalists* and *Emerging Consumers*. Again, the basic improvement in delivery has not affected the *Cape Coloured Emerging* group to the same extent as others because the most basic services were already available and thus improvement (i.e. performance relative to the past) has been greater elsewhere. The government's emphasis on primary health care provision and the HIV/AIDS controversy suggests that we can expect the most negative evaluations from the other two groups. As Table 26 shows, our expectations are confirmed.

Fighting corruption in government

Corruption in government has become a worldwide problem and a focus of organisations such as Transparency International. This is especially true of emerging economies and transitional societies.[2] South Africa has been no exception. The government has moved quickly to address issues of corruption, pursuing thousands of alleged incidents of corruption in the police force for example. The media has paid extensive attention to allegations of corruption concerning the granting of weapons contracts. The granting of the third cellular licence also attracted much attention as allegations of corruption were bandied about. Public perceptions of corruption

Table 26: *Providing basic health services*

Providing basic health services: how well would you say the government is handling this?

Group	Very well %	Fairly well %	Not very well %	Not at all well %	Don't know %	Refused %
Agrarian Lifestyles	23.4	51.0	15.9	8.7	1.0	
Border Survivalists	34.6	46.4	12.2	6.8		
Highveld Survivalists	29.3	45.1	19.5	5.7	0.4	
KZN Survivalists	23.0	49.7	16.0	9.4	1.9	
Free State Emerging	44.2	36.5	17.7	1.6		
Matchbox Suburban Youth	33.7	49.4	10.3	6.4	0.2	
Gauteng Township Youth	41.8	45.9	8.6	3.5	0.1	0.1
Cape Coloured Emerging	6.3	45.7	34.4	13.0	0.6	
Prime Skills	38.1	40.3	16.3	5.0	0.3	
East Coast Settlers	7.1	44.6	20.2	27.6		0.5
The Believers	3.3	23.6	26.2	46.3		0.6
Suburban Bliss	9.5	41.4	25.3	23.0		0.7
Suburban Challenge	8.5	26.8	30.4	33.7	0.7	
Earth Mothers	5.4	26.8	24.4	43.4		
Family Focus	6.9	19.8	27.8	43.4		2.1
Achievers	3.6	22.1	29.4	44.4	0.5	
National Average	25.8	42.8	18.0	12.9	0.5	0.1

have been heightened even more by revelations about corruption in the previous government that emerged from the Truth and Reconciliation Commission hearings.

The South African media has stated its belief repeatedly that focusing attention on corruption in the public sector is one of the most important jobs of a free press. Government has repeatedly called for what it believes is a more balanced presentation of such issues. Whatever your position in this debate, there is little doubt that the public has been widely sensitised to the problem of corruption.

It is beyond the scope of a book such as this to discuss the political issues surrounding corruption. It does, however, seem reasonable to assume that all of the attention paid to corruption in recent years – even if unproved or disproved – can be expected to leave most South Africans with the perception that their country has long-standing experience of corruption in government, and that it may well be going on today. Those who are most

Table 27: *Fighting corruption in government*

Fighting corruption in government: how well would you say the government is handling this?

Group	Very well %	Fairly well %	Not very well %	Not at all well %	Don't know %	Refused %
Agrarian Lifestyles	16.8	41.2	22.4	8.4	11.2	
Border Survivalists	14.5	42.0	28.6	7.3	7.6	
Highveld Survivalists	26.0	37.5	20.8	12.0	3.7	
KZN Survivalists	7.3	25.2	27.5	30.1	9.9	
Free State Emerging	23.5	50.1	22.6	3.8		
Matchbox Suburban Youth	23.8	35.1	26.5	11.6	3.0	
Gauteng Township Youth	24.8	39.3	23.9	10.4	1.5	0.1
Cape Coloured Emerging	1.5	25.8	38.3	25.1	9.3	
Prime Skills	22.4	32.8	36.1	6.5	2.3	
East Coast Settlers	2.0	19.6	31.2	45.9	0.8	0.5
The Believers	0.8	8.0	30.0	58.5	2.1	0.6
Suburban Bliss	6.1	16.6	39.9	34.6	2.1	0.7
Suburban Challenge	3.6	19.2	28.4	48.9		
Earth Mothers	0.6	19.7	30.7	47.2	1.7	
Family Focus	3.9	5.7	31.3	57.0	2.1	
Achievers	2.3	11.0	27.9	58.3	0.5	
National Average	15.8	32.3	27.1	20.0	4.6	0.1

literate and media-aware can be expected to be the most negative about the government's fight against corruption in its own ranks.

Table 27 shows the results. *Emerging Consumers* are once again more likely to have favourable perceptions of the government's performance and the *Urban Elite* are the least positive. There are some interesting observations to be made. The *KZN Survivalists*, who are resident almost exclusively in KwaZulu-Natal, believe the government is not doing well. The reason for this perception is unclear. One could hypothesise that this is the result of a specific local government perception. We note that the press was paying attention to the spending habits of the highest provincial government officials at the time of the survey, which could underlie this response. One reviewer of this book at manuscript stage suggested it might be an out-group derogation effect derived from a feeling that Zulus are under-represented at national government level. If this result continues to be observed, then it suggests the government should investigate the underlying reasons for the perception.

Prime Skills is surprising in its positive response. They are among the most employed groups and reside in the Gauteng industrial and government service heartland. Eight out of ten understand English and Afrikaans. More than two-thirds claim to read and write in either or both languages. It is possible that many of them work for government bodies.

Political party support

Respondents were asked to indicate which party they would vote for if elections were held the next day. The results are shown in Tables 28 and 29. Table 28 includes the *Rural Survivalists* and *Emerging Consumers* and thus includes the preferences of 65% of the South African population. Table 29 reports the results for *Urban Middle Class* and *Urban Elite*, a much smaller but perhaps economically more powerful group.

Do the groups help explain voting choices? The answer to this question is apparent immediately as one compares the two tables. In Table 28, the African National Congress garners more than 80% of the vote in most cases and other political parties fight for the meagre crumbs left on the table. Even the *KZN Survivalists* – 20% of whom would not indicate a choice on the day perhaps because of the history of political violence in the province – throw the majority of their support toward the ANC (53.9% translates to 67.4% of those who indicated a party choice). *Cape Coloured Emerging* also deviates from the pattern of these two groups by supporting the New National Party. The Democratic Party enjoys much more widespread support in Table 29, and so does the New National Party – although it emerges as a much less preferred party than the DP in the present survey. It is unclear how the split of the NNP and DP will affect the perceptions of the various groups.

No other party really gathers substantial support at the national level in this survey and readers are urged to examine the detailed results presented in the tables. It is interesting that the *Urban Middle Class* appears to be the least decisive as regards its voting intentions, scoring more than twice the national average of 'don't know' and 'I will not vote' responses. It would seem that many people in these groups might feel that no political party is adequately representing their aspirations.

Is your family better off?

We close this chapter with a glimpse into the personal assessments the respondents make about their living circumstances, something that clearly

Table 28: *Voting intentions*

National elections: how would you vote if elections were held tomorrow?

Group	AMP	ACDP	ANC	AEB	AZAPO	DP	FA	FF
	%	%	%	%	%	%	%	%
Agrarian Lifestyles			82.6			0.7		
Border Survivalists		1.3	86.0			1.5		
Highveld Survivalists	0.1	0.3	82.5			1.0		
KZN Survivalists		0.8	53.9			1.6		
Free State Emerging			85.6			1.1		
Matchbox Suburban Youth		1.0	84.7				0.3	
Gauteng Township Youth		1.0	82.3		0.8	0.8		
Cape Coloured Emerging	1.4	1.3	28.8	0.1		6.6		0.5
Prime Skills		1.2	81.0		0.3	2.7		0.3

Table 29: *Voting intentions (continued)*

National elections: how would you vote if elections were held tomorrow?

Group	AMP	ACDP	ANC	AEB	AZAPO	DP	FA	FF
	%	%	%	%	%	%	%	%
East Coast Settlers	3.8	4.0	15.9			26.3		0.8
The Believers		4.5	5.0	1.6		37.5	1.6	4.5
Suburban Bliss		4.3	14.8	0.8		35.7	0.7	3.8
Suburban Challenge		4.4	15.3			37.7	0.7	2.6
Earth Mothers		6.5	5.2			48.7		1.9
Family Focus		3.5	3.4	2.1		56.5	0.7	2.1
Achievers		1.9	5.4			49.7	1.9	6.2
National Average	0.2	1.4	63.1	0.1	0.1	9.5	0.2	0.7

AMP – African Muslim Party
ACDP – African Christian Democratic Party
ANC – African National Congress
AEB – Afrikaner Eenheidsbeweging
AZAPO – Azanian People's Organisation
DP – Democratic Party
FA – Federal Alliance
FF – Freedom Front

IFP %	MF %	NP %	PAC %	UCDP %	UDM %	Other party %	Don't know %	I will not vote %	Spoilt ballot %	Refused %
7.2		0.5		0.2	1.1		4.2	0.5	0.6	2.3
		0.4	1.1		5.2		2.8	0.9	0.2	0.7
0.5		0.2	2.7	1.5	1.5		5.8	0.8	0.9	2.4
22.2		0.6		0.3	0.5		4.8	1.1	0.5	13.7
		1.4	4.1		1.0		3.6		1.1	2.1
0.9		2.1	1.1	1.5			3.4	0.3	2.0	2.6
2.0		0.9	1.7	0.5	0.8	0.2	5.0	1.4	0.6	2.0
0.4		44.2	0.4	0.4	3.0		7.6	2.7	0.6	1.8
1.0	0.3	0.8		0.9	6.9		2.6	0.9	0.1	0.9

IFP %	MF %	NP %	PAC %	UCDP %	UDM %	Other party %	Don't know %	I will not vote %	Spoilt ballot %	Refused %
1.3	2.3	17.0		1.5	2.5		10.7	3.3	1.0	9.5
1.3		16.5			1.3	0.5	13.5	3.3	0.5	8.0
0.7		18.4			1.3	1.3	12.0	3.5	1.5	1.3
		18.9		1.3	3.4	0.7	9.3	3.6	0.7	1.7
0.6		5.2			2.1		8.4	8.2	2.5	10.6
0.7		10.8			1.6	0.7	7.3	1.4	0.7	9.5
1.1		11.3		1.9	1.9		7.4	2.2	2.5	6.9
3.4	0.1	5.6	1.0	0.7	2.0	0.1	5.6	1.4	.9	4.2

IFP – Inkatha Freedom Party
MF – Minority Front
NP – New National Party
PAC – Pan Africanist Congress
UCDP – United Christian Democratic Party
UDM – United Democratic Movement

Table 30: *Better or worse off than last year*

Thinking of the way your family lives, would you say that your family is ...?

Group	Better off than a year ago %	About the same %	Worse off than a year ago %
Agrarian Lifestyles	23.6	57.0	19.4
Border Survivalists	33.2	53.0	13.7
Highveld Survivalists	28.3	56.6	15.1
KZN Survivalists	23.0	47.5	29.6
Free State Emerging	24.1	62.6	13.3
Matchbox Suburban Youth	34.6	47.6	17.7
Gauteng Township Youth	31.9	48.3	19.8
Cape Coloured Emerging	35.7	41.5	22.8
Prime Skills	46.9	46.2	6.8
East Coast Settlers	37.9	40.4	21.7
The Believers	20.8	47.0	32.3
Suburban Bliss	39.7	46.3	14.0
Suburban Challenge	36.7	39.3	24.0
Earth Mothers	29.6	49.0	21.4
Family Focus	21.8	58.3	19.9
Achievers	40.6	40.6	18.9
National Average	30.8	50.6	18.6

impacts on their political attitudes and voting choices. We begin by exploring how they feel their family is living when compared to how they lived a year ago.

In general, the vast majority of South Africans felt that life was the same or better than last year. *Prime Skills*, the most educated group comprised mostly of black South Africans, is the most positive about their life versus last year. However, they are not really all that unique as more than 80% of the groups who enjoy the highest levels of human development report that life is the same or better.

The most negative perception of life is reported by a group that is comprised primarily of whites. *The Believers* have the least economic resources of any group comprised primarily of whites. They are one of only two groups in which less people claim life is better than those who claim it is worse. One in three respondents claims life is worse. The *KZN Survivalists* is the other group that feels life is generally worse. Although more than 80% saw

Table 31: *One year on*

And how do you think it will be in a year's time? Do you think your family will be …?

Group	Better off than a year ago %	About the same %	Worse off than a year ago %	Don't know %
Agrarian Lifestyles	32.3	52.8	11.7	3.2
Border Survivalists	38.6	50.7	8.4	2.3
Highveld Survivalists	49.0	39.1	10.6	1.3
KZN Survivalists	25.3	46.4	24.3	4.0
Free State Emerging	52.4	38.8	7.7	1.1
Matchbox Suburban Youth	48.2	41.1	9.5	1.2
Gauteng Township Youth	47.2	37.9	13.1	1.8
Cape Coloured Emerging	52.9	34.4	8.8	3.8
Prime Skills	51.7	39.6	5.5	3.2
East Coast Settlers	37.5	44.0	14.5	4.0
The Believers	23.2	43.6	31.3	1.9
Suburban Bliss	47.6	44.2	8.2	
Suburban Challenge	43.0	44.0	13.0	
Earth Mothers	33.9	52.6	12.8	0.6
Family Focus	15.6	68.8	14.9	0.7
Achievers	33.0	51.6	14.4	0.9
National Average	41.2	44.2	12.4	2.1

improvement or no change, *Family Focus* is the second most likely to claim that life has not improved.

So the general picture that emerges in Table 30 is that life has stayed the same or improved when compared to a year ago but some people clearly perceive life to be worse, and that it will get worse still in the future.

How will life be next year?

Table 31 shows the response to a query about how life would be one year from the day of the interview. The response is much more positive. Overall, one-third more people feel that life will be better in a year than those who feel life was better than last year. *The Believers* and the *KZN Survivalists* remain the least positive. Although only one in seven feel that life will be worse in a year's time, *Family Focus* is the only group of which fewer people believe life will be better next year, when compared to the proportion that felt life was better than the previous year. They are more likely to be of retirement age and perhaps more likely to be living on fixed income.

The greatest gains are observed among the *Emerging Consumers* and *Rural Survivalists*. *Highveld Survivalists* and *Free State Emerging* rise more than 20 points when compared to Table 30. This represents at least a 75% gain in both cases. The proportion of most groups in the top box (i.e. 'better' category) increases some 20%. A most positive picture from a country that is supposed to be dogged by pessimism!

Closing comments

In this chapter, we explored the political attitudes, voting intentions and worldview of the 16 tribes as defined in the SA Tribes research project. The results show that SA Tribes helps explain how people act politically and why they act as they do. The results reveal a positive picture generally. Nonetheless, the results for the *KZN Survivalists*, the *Cape Coloured Emerging* and *The Believers* – groups with a strong ethnic identity who sit on the bottom rung of their respective Apartheid race groups – show that some are less satisfied with life. In the following chapter, we conclude by highlighting some key findings that have emerged from the SA Tribes research programme and consider their implications for government and private sector organisations.

8: Closing thoughts
How to live happily ever after

SA Tribes began as a study to help South African companies understand how South Africans were changing and what the commercial implications of that change were. As our research unfolded, it confirmed our tentative thoughts about the power of social identity in explaining human behaviour and understanding social change. In the preceding chapters, we briefly reviewed theories concerning identity and its main elements, proposed a theory of identity influence, developed a typology of South African identity types, explored primary identifications in 11 sub-Saharan African nations and showed how the SA Tribes programme helps explain differences in consumer and political behaviour. The results show the impressive benefits that can be achieved when one thinks of people as dynamic and complex identities who behave in response to the situations in which they find themselves, rather than as members of fixed racial groups.

This chapter presents some closing thoughts about the implications of our findings. We address the commercial and political implications first, and then discuss some general implications for individuals in South Africa.

What business must do

Firms that develop an empathetic understanding of consumers (i.e. a market orientation) have been shown to increase their chances for marketing success and shareholder value substantially.[1] Organisations that understand consumer identities will benefit most because their knowledge gives them the power to craft winning strategies that enrich all of their stakeholders, especially their customers. Simply put, they are more at one with their entire marketplace and all its members.

In this section we discuss a methodology for developing a constantly renewable understanding of consumers using the model of identity influence. The model of identity influence that was introduced in Chapter 3 is reproduced on page 114 and forms the basis of our discussion.

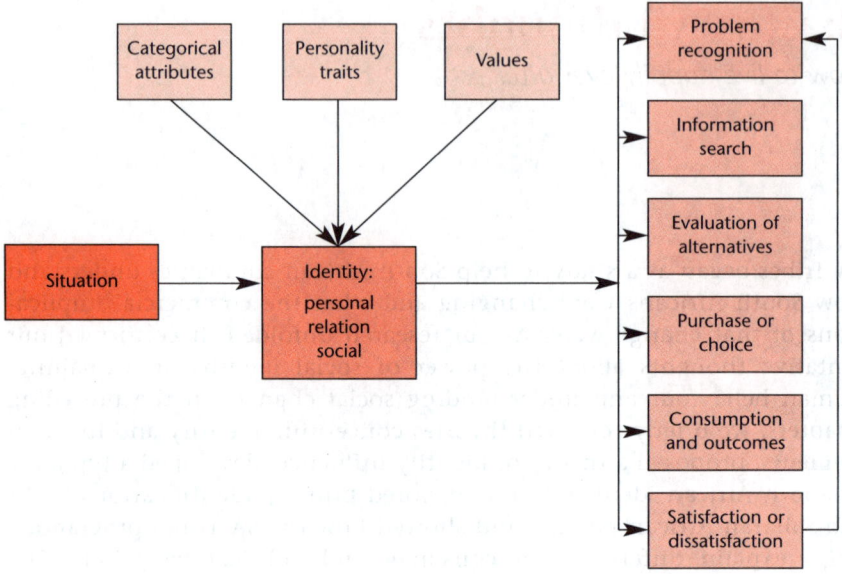

Figure 7: *The SA Tribes model of identity influence*

Developing a market orientation

Market orientation is about three things: (1) acquiring information about customer problems, (2) making sense of those problems and sharing knowledge about them throughout the organisation and (3) developing and implementing strategies that respond to consumer needs and solve their problems. Even companies such as wholesalers, who may not deal directly with the public, must understand the purchase and consumption behaviour of that final market if they are to be successful supply-chain members. It all sounds so very simple in concept but even the most market-driven firms find that it can be difficult to achieve a truly lasting and vibrant market orientation.

The starting point is to consider the communication, purchase and consumption situations in which people are most likely to find themselves. The four higher order groups and the 16 tribal groups can be a useful starting point in this process because they paint a portrait of the basic situations and living circumstances in which people spend their time and money. However, it is not enough to understand the basic issue that *Rural Survivalists* and *Urban Elites* live very different lives and act on purchase and consumption impulses within very different situations. More information is needed.

This implies the need for additional qualitative and quantitative research.[2] Although the approach presented in *SA Tribes* has been a quantitative, survey-based approach, there is a need for more qualitative research as well. Focus-groups, in-depth interviews, laddering and other projective techniques may uncover rich, motivational information that helps explain the functional and psychosocial benefits people receive from varied product offerings. Quantitative research will also be needed to 'count heads', prior to charging off in potentially the wrong direction. The results of qualitative research are generally not really capable of being projected onto the market – due to the small sample sizes and lack of representativeness that often characterise the respondents.

If identity is the starting place, then one must carefully consider the various identities that come into play (i.e. relational, personal and social) and the human characteristics that comprise it (i.e. the values, traits, awareness of race or living standards, etc.). This knowledge then needs to be considered carefully at each stage of the consumer decision process.[3]

Problem recognition

Thinking of a person as having needs often leads to the erroneous conclusion that the objective of marketing is to create a need. Needs, of course, cannot be created: they already exist. Even if a firm focuses on needs, the overall strategy must be to activate a need by helping the customer realise they have it. In any event, I prefer an alternative way of thinking: one that leads to greater marketing success.

I believe in thinking of customers as problem-solvers. Problem recognition is the most important stage of the consumer decision process. As with needs, if consumers don't recognise problems then they don't seek solutions. Making the shift to thinking about people as problem-solvers opens the door to many potential advantages. First, it creates an atmosphere in which everyone in the firm can begin to understand their role in customer interactions – and understand that role from the customer's point-of-view. Second, they begin to see their role as problem-solvers. This opens the door to a pervasive, company-wide culture that is truly empathetic, responsive and market-oriented. People who do business with such firms feel that they are understood, appreciated and well-served. The SA Tribes groupings are important because they contextualise the background environment from which consumers' problems emerge.

There are many problems on which the company must focus. What problems does a consumer with this identity recognise? Why? What is their perception of their current circumstances as regards the problem? What is their perception of the ideal state that they might be able to afford based on their cognitive, time and monetary resources?

People often misjudge their actual circumstances or are unaware of just how much better things could be. People will not buy a product (i.e. the bundle of solutions the firm offers) unless its cognitive, time and monetary cost is deemed to be reasonable in terms of the benefits it delivers. This implies three strategies are open to the firm: help people see their true current state, help them see how much better things could really be, help them see the true cost of solving the problem. All of these strategies will be different for the different SA Tribes groupings.

Providing the right solution

Once consumers recognise a problem that needs solving, they set out to solve it. One can immediately see the value of SA Tribes for conceptualising how organisations should respond strategically to the varied media consumption habits. This ranges from *Rural Survivalists*, who depend mainly on verbal communication with others and on radio, to the *Urban Elite*, who consult a wide range of local and international media. Again, each group will clearly have different needs that require careful consideration.

The considerations are not only of media placement. Many products that would not be considered innovative require very innovative behaviour on the part of *Rural Survivalists* or *Emerging Consumers*.

It is necessary to understand the current knowledge and perceptions people hold and their ability to associate brand images and content. What is the content and extent of product knowledge? Is the product something completely new to this person's lifestyle? What does it replace? Where do consumers such as this look for information? What product criteria do they evaluate and which are most influential in their decision? Who else will influence them and what characteristics do those influential people have that cause them to be influential and to recognise the problems and solutions they do?

It is also worth remembering that the importance of a physically attractive model to appear in advertisements and promotional communications may be outweighed by his or her similarity to the target audience. Similarity can substantially enhance an advertisement's persuasiveness.

Purchase and its outcomes

Once people realise that they want something, they have to find a place to buy it. Spaza shops and other informal sector outlets have attracted a lot of attention during the last decade. Network marketing – as is practised by Avon, Justine, Herbalife, Amway, Golden Products and a host of other fast-growth firms – is another alternative that seems well placed for the more economically challenged groups. Network marketing offers real advantages because it creates employment and substantially cuts distribution costs.

There are many more questions to answer. Where do they believe they will find the product for purchase? At what price and with what features? How will they use it? Dispose of it? And so on. There must be interplay of identity and decision at each stage of the process. This iterative approach should continue constantly in a company, as I pointed out in *The New Marketing*.[4] Firms that pursue such an approach will no doubt find success in South Africa and beyond.

Identity in the firm

Of course, the influence of identity is not only external to the firm. Identity, like culture, is a silent influence that people do not notice because it is always present. Every associate in the firm must be sensitised to identity issues. This is not to suggest that associates with a firm should attempt to associate every customer and potential customer with an SA Tribe identity. However, knowledge of the SA Tribes groupings will help associates better understand the people with whom they come into contact. Establishing internal discussion groups that include people from all levels within the company (shop floor industrial workers, middle management, executives, etc.) not only makes sense from the perspective of company unity, it also allows people in close contact with some of these communities to share their knowledge of them. It turns everyone into a mentor and a learner. Firms that can establish and nurture such a culture will develop an incredibly strong market orientation throughout the firm. They will probably experience fewer labour problems also!

What government must do

There are many case studies that show how identity can knit together disparate people in a newly constituted nation – as was the case in the United States and Singapore – and lead to social stability and progress. However, there is plenty of evidence in every corner of the world to prove that identity can also lead to behaviour that excludes, discriminates, aggresses and tears at the very fabric of society. If we consider the most heinous crimes against humanity from the dawn of recorded history, we witness crimes that were instigated in most cases by one group trying to exercise preferential rights over another. Race, tribe, religion, social class, home language and culture are among the many inconsequential human differences that have been manufactured into meaningful reasons so that people might kill one another.

But identity also has a very positive aspect. South Africa is unusually fortunate to have such widespread positive opinions about the present and future, as emerge in this study. Our results suggest that South Africans generally find today to be better than yesterday and expect tomorrow to be a better place than today. There are, however, signs of groups that are experiencing turmoil and feelings of being left out. Some require intensive investigation now to determine the cause of their more negative perceptions. The 'South African miracle' is by no means secure and there is no reason for complacency. There is much to do.

The socio-political implications of SA Tribes for government leaders are as immediately apparent as the commercial realities. South Africa's motto – unity in diversity – implies a deep understanding of social identity. For unity in diversity to occur, there must be diversity. It is a tacit recognition that escapes many people, a recognition that no matter how unified this country becomes there will always be people who celebrate their differences and seek out others who share their unique characteristics. Different social identities need not impair the ability to form a greater national identity.

Group identity is a repulsive notion to many people in government because it churns up the bitter memories of the forced racial identities of the Apartheid years. One reason for the length of the theory chapter earlier in this book is to allow readers to establish for themselves the incredible complexity of identity. Although it would be fair to say that the 16 SA Tribes seem to differ based on racial and geographic identity, the results of the research show that living standards are the most important influence on their identity. SA Tribes makes it very clear that identity groups are much more complex than simple groups based on Apartheid-era racial identities. The great paradox is that in order to build a sense of national identity – one that rises above race, ethnicity, gender and other human characteristics – government leaders must be careful not to challenge existing identities. In time, being white or Coloured or whatever will lose its meaning and these group identities will disappear on their own, perhaps even within a generation. Shared schools and other institutions will be most effective in bringing people together as South Africans. Among the most important things that government can do – according to social identity theory – is to identify goals that everyone in South Africa can endorse and share in working towards.

Emphasising the construction of a layer of inclusive identity for everyone as a South African is the best way to overcome the legacy of more than 100 years of enforced separate racial identities. Gaining wide agreement about and commitment to national goals would be an important step toward building that sense of shared identity.

Research programmes should be mounted to study identity and develop a better understanding of its influences within different regions and groups of people. Government departments that address the softer issues such as arts and culture need to ascertain the effectiveness of these mediums to stimulate knowledge about identity. Programmes should be developed by government, business and communities that provide a platform for shared knowledge-building about identity. Particular interest should be focused on helping business understand the more economically challenged groups, so that upliftment programmes can be more effective. South Africa's competitive advantage would be enhanced, thereby creating more jobs in the economy as that knowledge is applied in other emerging economies. Business will not readily see the advantages of sitting for days in 'talk shops'; government must be sensitive to breaking out of bureaucracy and moving to more active research, strategy and implementation.

What individuals must do

My final comments are directed to individuals. Every South African has a stake in a peaceful and prosperous South Africa. It is imperative that people take the time to engage one another. This implies the greatest challenge to those in the most economically developed groups. Paying taxes is not enough. What South Africa needs is buy-in for a national identity. That cannot happen unless our most influential people come to understand and value the identities of those less fortunate. I know that I do not make enough effort on most days to understand people who are very dissimilar to me and I suspect that many people who read this book will adjudge themselves in a similar fashion.

There is nothing that a truly unified South Africa cannot do. I leave you with a quotation from the Baha'í writings: 'The Earth is but one country and humankind its citizens.' The challenge for every South African is to make such a dream a reality!

Notes

Chapter 1

[1] George Herbert Mead: *Mind, Self and Society* (University of Chicago Press, 1934).

[2] Chapter 2 briefly reviews some of this research to establish the theoretical rationale for this study.

[3] Bill Clinton: 'The Struggle for the Soul of the 21st Century.' Paper presented at the Dimbleby Lecture, London, 14 December 2001.

[4] Henri Tajfel: 'Social Identity and Intergroup Behavior.' *Social Science Information* 13, no. 2 (1974). Henri Tajfel, ed.: *The Social Dimension: European Studies in Social Psychology*, 2 vols. (Cambridge University Press, 1984). Henri Tajfel and J. C. Turner: 'An Integrative Theory of Intergroup Conflict', in *The Social Psychology of Intergroup Relations*, ed. W. G. Austin and S. Worchel (Brooks/Cole, 1979).

[5] E. Tory Higgins: 'The 'Self Digest': Self-Knowledge Serving Self-Regulatory Functions', *Journal of Personality and Social Psychology* 71, no. 6 (1996).

[6] For example, the great personality researcher Robert R. McCrae recently argued that '… virtually the entire body of research on personality can be considered an intracultural study of personality in Western societies … comparative intracultural studies (are) needed …' Robert R. McCrae: 'Trait Psychology and the Revival of Personality and Culture Studies', *American Behavioral Scientist* 44, no. 1 (2000). Kent B. Monroe: 'Editorial', *Journal of Consumer Research* 19, no. 4 (1993), and John A. Quelch and James E. Austin: 'Should Multinationals Invest in Africa?' *Sloan Management Review* 34, no. 3 (1993), make similar arguments.

Chapter 2

[1] Max Yasgur's farm was the site of the famous Woodstock concert. Crosby, Stills, Nash & Young originally released *Almost Cut My Hair* and the hit *Woodstock*, 11 March 1970 on the Déjà Vu album.

[2] Sourced at http://www.pollstar.com/toptours.htm for the week ending 5 January 2002.

[3] Higgins: 'The 'Self Digest': Self-Knowledge Serving Self-Regulatory Functions.'

[4] H. Markus: 'Self-Schemata and Processing Information About the Self', *Journal of Personality and Social Psychology* 35, no. 1 (1977).

[5] Marilynn B. Brewer and Wendi L. Gardner: 'Who Is This 'We'? Levels of Collective Identity and Self-Representations', *Journal of Personality and Social Psychology* 71 (1996).

[6] Morris Rosenberg: *Conceiving the Self* (Basic Books, 1979).

[7] Henri Tajfel: *Differentiation between Social Groups: Studies in the Social Psychology of Intergroup Relations* (Academic Press, 1978), 63.

[8] See Abebe Zegeye: 'Imposed Ethnicity', in *Social Identities in the New South Africa*, ed. Abebe Zegeye (Kwela Books, 2001).

[9] Excellent reviews are provided by Marilynn B. Brewer and Rupert J. Brown: 'Intergroup Relations', in *The Handbook of Social Psychology*, ed. Daniel T. Gilbert, Susan T. Fiske and Gardner Lindzey (McGraw-Hill, 1998); Carmel Camilleri and Hanna Malewska-Peyre: 'Socialization and Identity Strategies', in *Handbook of Cross-Cultural Psychology*, ed. John W. Berry, Pierre R. Dasen and T. S. Saraswati (Allyn and Bacon, 1997); William B. Gudykunst and Michael Harris Bond: 'Intergroup Relations across Cultures', in *Handbook of Cross-Cultural Psychology*, ed. John W. Berry, Marshall H. Segall and Cigdem Kagitçibasi (Allyn and Bacon, 1997).

[10] See M. Hogg and D. Abrams: *Social Identifications* (Routledge, 1988); Tajfel: 'Social Identity and Intergroup Behavior.'

[11] For instance, George A. Kelly: *A Theory of Personality: The Psychology of Personal Constructs* (Norton, 1950); Carl R. Rogers: *On Becoming a Person: A Therapist's View of Psychotherapy* (Constable, 1967).

[12] See Milton Rokeach: 'Inducing Change and Stability in Belief Systems and Personality Structures', *Journal of Social Issues* 41, no. 1 (1985).

[13] For instance, Mead: *Mind, Self and Society*; Muzafer Sherif: *The Psychology of Social Norms* (Harper Row, 1936).

[14] Camilleri and Malewska-Peyre: 'Socialization and Identity Strategies.'

[15] Linda A. Jackson et al.: 'Achieving Positive Social Identity: Social Mobility, Social Creativity and Permeability of Group Boundaries', *Journal of Personality and Social Psychology* 70, no. 2 (1996).

[16] William Sumner, a free market economist and social Darwinist, called attention to the distinction and its implications for in-group favouritism in his last major work before he died, William Graham Sumner: *Folkways* (Ginn, 1906).

[17] Henri Tajfel: *Human Groups and Social Categories: Studies in Social Psychology* (Cambridge University Press, 1981).

[18] Henri Tajfel: 'Experiments in Intergroup Discrimination', *Scientific American* 223, no. 2 (1970).

[19] Tajfel and Turner: 'An Integrative Theory of Intergroup Conflict.'

[20] Tajfel: *Human Groups and Social Categories: Studies in Social Psychology*.

[21] Muzafer Sherif: *Group Conflict and Co-Operation: Their Social Psychology* (Routledge and Kegan Paul, 1966).

[22] Naomi Struch and Shalom H. Schwartz: 'Intergroup Aggression: Its Predictors and Distinctness from In-Group Bias', *Journal of Personality and Social Psychology* 56, no. 3 (1989).

[23] Camilleri and Malewska-Peyre: 'Socialization and Identity Strategies'; Michael Hooper: 'The Structure and Measurement of Social Identity', *Public Opinion Quarterly* 40, no. 2 (1976).

[24] Briefly reviewed in Susan T. Fiske: 'Stereotyping, Prejudice, and Discrimination' in *The Handbook of Social Psychology*, ed. Daniel T. Gilbert, Susan T. Fiske and Gardner Lindzey (McGraw Hill, 1998).

[25] For instance, see P. G. Devine: 'Stereotypes and Prejudice: Their Automatic and Controlled Components', *Journal of Personality and Social Psychology* 56 (1989).

[26] Marilynn B. Brewer: 'In-group Bias in the Minimal Intergroup Situation: A Cognitive-Motivational Analysis', *Psychological Bulletin* 86 (1979).

[27] See Richard L. Allen, Michael C. Dawson and Ronald E. Brown: 'A Schema-Based Approach to Modeling an African-American Racial Belief System', *American Political Science Review* 83, no. 2 (1989); Monica Biernat et al.: 'Values and Prejudice: Toward Understanding the Impact of American Values on Outgroup Attitudes', in *The Psychology of Values: The Ontario Symposium*, ed. Clive Seligman, James M. Olson and Mark P. Zanna (Lawrence Erlbaum, 1996); Jim Blascovich et al.: 'Racism and Racial Categorization', *Journal of Personality and Social Psychology* 72, no. 6 (1997); Clifford L. Broman, Harold W. Neighbors and James S. Jackson: 'Racial Group Identification among Black Adults', *Social Forces* 67, no. 1 (1988), Devine: 'Stereotypes and Prejudice: Their Automatic and Controlled Components'; Steven Fein and Steven J. Spencer: 'Prejudice as Self-Image Maintenance: Affirming the Self through Derogating Others', *Social Psychology* 73, no. 1 (1997); Fiske: 'Stereotyping, Prejudice, and Discrimination'; G. A. Tyson, Anne Schlachter and Saths Cooper: 'Game Playing Strategy as an Indicator of Racial Prejudice among South African Students', *The Journal of Social Psychology* 128, no. 4 (1987); Graham M. Vaughan: 'Social Change and Racial Identity: Issues in the Use of Picture and Doll Measures', *Australian Journal of Psychology* 38, no. 3 (1986); Maykel Verkuyten and Louk Hagendoorn: 'Prejudice and Self-Categorization: The Variable Role of Authoritarianism and In-Group Stereotypes', *Personality and Social Psychology Bulletin* 24, no. 1 (1998).

[28] Camilleri and Malewska-Peyre: 'Socialization and Identity Strategies.'

[29] G. W. Allport and H. S. Odbert: 'Trait Names: A Psycho-Lexical Study', *Psychological Monograms* 47, no. 1 (1936).

[30] So called because factors are produced using exploratory factor analysis, a multi-dimensional statistical analysis technique that identifies underlying factors that help explain underlying patterns in data.

[31] For a more detailed discussion of OSL, see Hans Baumgartner and Jan-Benedict E. M. Steenkamp: 'Exploratory Consumer Behaviour: Conceptualization and Measurement', *International Journal of Research in Marketing* 13, no. 2 (1996); Jan-Benedict E. M. Steenkamp and Hans Baumgartner: 'Development and Cross-Cultural Validation of a Short Form Csi as a Measure of Optimum Stimulation Level', *International Journal of Research in Marketing* 12, no. 2 (1995); Jan-Benedict E. M. Steenkamp and Hans Baumgartner: 'The Role of Optimum Stimulation Level in Exploratory Consumer Behavior', *Journal of Consumer Research* 19, no. 3 (1992); Jan-Benedict E. M. Steenkamp and Steven M. Burgess: 'Optimum Stimulation Level and Exploratory Consumer Behaviour in an Emerging Consumer Market', *International Journal of Research in Marketing* 19 (2002); Jan-Benedict E. M. Steenkamp, Hans Baumgartner and Elise Van der Wulp: 'Arousal Potential, Arousal, Stimulus Attractiveness, and the Moderating Role of Need for Stimulation', *International Journal of Research in Marketing* 13, no. 4 (1996).

[32] Zuckerman has linked OSL to levels of monoamineoxidase in the brain, see Marvin Zuckerman: *Behavioral Expressions and Biosocial Bases of Sensation Seeking* (Cambridge University Press, 1994); Marvin Zuckerman: *Sensation Seeking: Beyond the Optimal Level of Arousal* (Lawrence Erlbaum, 1979). It is still far too early to suggest a genetic link although some work is encouraging, see R. P. Ebstein et al.: 'Additional Evidence for an Association between the Dopamine D4 Receptor (D4dr) Exon Iii Repeat Polymorphism and the Human Personality Trait of Novelty Seeking', *Molecular Psychiatry* 2, no. 6 (1997); R. P. Ebstein et al.: 'Dopamine D4 Receptor (D4dr) Exon Iii Polymorphism Associated with the Human Personality Trait of Novelty Seeking', *Nature Genetics* 12 (1996).

[33] P. S. Raju: 'Optimum Stimulation Level: Its Relationship to Personality, Demographics, and Exploratory Behavior', *Journal of Consumer Research* 7, no. December (1980).

[34] For instance, see Rogers' seminal tome, Everitt Rogers: *Diffusion of Innovations* (The Free Press, 1962).

[35] Steven M. Burgess and Mari Harris: 'High and Low Optimum Stimulation Level Consumers: Their Characteristics, Living Standards, Lifestyle Interests, and Product Choice Behaviors' (paper presented at the Academy of Marketing Science Multicultural Marketing Conference, Montreal, 1998); Steven M. Burgess and Mari Harris: 'Values, Optimum Stimulation Levels and Brand Loyalty: New Scales in New Populations', *South African Journal of Business Management* 29, no. 4 (1998).

[36] Frankl is the father of logotherapy and was among the most seminal contributors to the humanist approach to psychology. His books continue to be popular and are available in most South African bookstores, see Victor E. Frankl: *The Doctor and the Soul* (Knopf, 1955); Victor E. Frankl: *Man's Search for Meaning* (Beacon, 1959).

[37] John L. Lastovicka: 'On the Validation of Lifestyle Traits: A Review and Illustration', *Journal of Marketing Research* 19, no. 1 (1982); Donald E. Vinson, Jerome Scott, E., and Lawrence M. Lamont: 'The Role of Personal Values in Marketing and Consumer Behavior', *Journal of Marketing*, no. April (1977).

[38] Burgess and Harris: 'Values, Optimum Stimulation Levels and Brand Loyalty: New Scales in New Populations.'

[39] For a more detailed comparison of values and traits, see Steven M. Burgess: 'Personal Values and Consumer Research: An Historical Perspective', in *Research in Marketing*, ed. Jagdish N. Sheth (JAI Press, 1992); David G. Winter et al.: 'Traits and Motives: Toward an Integration of Two Traditions in Personality Research', *Psychological Review* 105, no. 2 (1998).

[40] Shalom H. Schwartz et al.: 'Extending the Cross-Cultural Validity of the Theory of Basic Human Values with a Different Method of Measurement', *Journal of Cross-Cultural Psychology* 32, no. 5 (2001).

[41] Lastovicka: 'On the Validation of Lifestyle Traits: A Review and Illustration.'

[42] Milton Rokeach: *The Nature of Human Values* (Free Press, 1973); Milton Rokeach: *Understanding Human Values* (Free Press, 1979).

[43] See the discussion in Burgess: 'Personal Values and Consumer Research: An Historical Perspective.'

44 For example, Steven M. Burgess, Shalom H. Schwartz and Roger D. Blackwell: 'Do Values Share Universal Content and Structure? A South African Test', *South African Journal of Psychology* 24, no. 1 (1994); Steven M. Burgess and Jan-Benedict E. M. Steenkamp: 'Value Priorities and Consumer Behavior in a Transitional Economy: The Case of South Africa', in *Marketing Issues in Transitional Economies*, ed. Rajeev Batra (Kluwer Academic Press, 1999); Schwartz et al.: 'Extending the Cross-Cultural Validity of the Theory of Basic Human Values with a Different Method of Measurement.'

45 Schwartz et al.: 'Extending the Cross-Cultural Validity of the Theory of Basic Human Values with a Different Method of Measurement.'

46 Shalom Schwartz: 'Universals in the Content and Structure of Values: Theoretical Advances and Empirical Tests in 20 Countries', *Advances in Experimental Social Psychology* 25 (1992); Shalom H. Schwartz: 'Are There Universal Aspects in the Content and Structure of Human Values?', *Journal of Social Issues* 50, no. 4 (1994); Schwartz et al.: 'Extending the Cross-Cultural Validity of the Theory of Basic Human Values with a Different Method of Measurement.'

47 Scale use is a form of bias that is well documented in the cross-cultural psychology literature and has been noted by Schwartz as a problem in values research. Scale use bias occurs when one population uses a scale differently, for instance, being more likely generally to agree with all items on a questionnaire even when items have opposing meaning. This could be because one population is more likely to agree with statements on a questionnaire out of courtesy (the so-called courtesy bias), to demonstrate competency to the interviewer or for other reasons. Professional research companies train interviewers to minimise such bias and researchers spend much time designing reliable and valid measures so that data can be relied on to indicate real differences. As we detail later, procedures were put in place to detect scale use bias in the present values research and thus these respondents are removed for the OSL results as well.

48 See Burgess: 'Personal Values and Consumer Research: An Historical Perspective.'

49 Jan-Benedict E. M. Steenkamp, Frankel ter Hofstede and Michel Wedel: 'A Cross-National Investigation into the Individual and Cultural Antecedents of Consumer Innovativeness', *Journal of Marketing Research* 36, no. February (1999).

50 For instance, see Steven M. Burgess and Roger D. Blackwell: 'Evaluations of Non-celebrities in Print Ads: An Exploratory Study on the Influence of Source Attractiveness, Similarity and Consumer Values' (Graduate School of Business Working Paper Series, University of Cape Town, 2000).

51 At Ohio State the headline was changed to: 'Before Nordic Ice, she was Mommy's 'good little girl' down at OSU' because of meaning issues (e.g. marks are called grades in the USA). Our thanks to Nordic Ice for permission to use their excellent advertisement and to reproduce it here.

52 R. B. Cialdini, C. A. Kallgren, and R. R. Reno: 'A Focus Theory on Normative Conduct: A Theoretical Refinement and Reevaluation of the Role of Norms in Human Behavior', *Advances in Experimental Social Psychology* 21 (1991).

53 Shalom H. Schwartz: 'Normative Influence on Altruism', in *Advances in Experimental Social Psychology*, ed. L. Berkowitz (Academic Press, 1977).

⁵⁴ Individualism and collectivism are reviewed in greater detail by Harry C. Triandis: *Individualism and Collectivism* (Westview Press, 1995); Harry C. Triandis et al.: 'The Measurement of the Etic Aspects of Individualism and Collectivism across Cultures', *Australian Journal of Psychology* 38, no. 3 (1986); Harry C. Triandis, Christopher McCusker and C. Harry Hui: 'Multimethod Probes of Individualism and Collectivism', *Journal of Personality and Social Psychology* 59, no. November (1990). Idiocentrism and allocentrism are the individual level equivalents of individualism and collectivism, see Harry C. Triandis et al.: 'Allocentric Versus Idiocentric Tendencies: Convergent and Discriminant Validation', *Journal of Research in Personality* 19 (1985).

⁵⁵ Triandis, McCusker and Hui: 'Multimethod Probes of Individualism and Collectivism.'

⁵⁶ ibid.

⁵⁷ ibid.

⁵⁸ Shalom H. Schwartz and Maria Ros: 'Values in the West: A Theoretical and Empirical Challenge to the Individualism-Collectivism Cultural Dimension', *World Psychology* 1, no. 2 (1995).

⁵⁹ Nan M. Sussman: 'The Dynamic Nature of Cultural Identity Throughout Cultural Transitions: Why Home Is Not So Sweet', *Personality and Social Psychology Review* 4, no. 4 (2000).

Chapter 3

¹ United Nations Development Programme: 'Human Development Report 2000: Human Rights and Human Development' (Oxford University Press, 2000).

² Rajeev Batra: 'Marketing Issues and Challenges in Transitional Economies', in *Marketing Issues in Transitional Economies*, ed. Rajeev Batra (Kluwer Academic Press, 1999).

³ See W. K. Garlington and H. E. Shimota: 'The Change Seeker Index: A Measure of the Need for Variable Stimulus Input', *Psychological Reports* 14 (1964); Steenkamp and Baumgartner: 'The Role of Optimum Stimulation Level in Exploratory Consumer Behavior.'

⁴ Hans and Jan-Benedict E. M. Steenkamp Baumgartner: 'Multi-Group Latent Variable Models for Varying Numbers of Items and Factors with Cross-National and Longitudinal Applications', *Marketing Letters* 9, no. 1 (1998); Steenkamp and Baumgartner: 'Development and Cross-Cultural Validation of a Short Form Csi as a Measure of Optimum Stimulation Level.'

⁵ Extensive information is provided about the cross-cultural measurement invariance of the CSI scale in the present research using a more and more restricted confirmatory factor analysis (structural equation modelling) approach in Steenkamp and Burgess: 'Optimum Stimulation Level and Exploratory Consumer Behaviour in an Emerging Consumer Market.'

⁶ Shalom H. Schwartz, Arielle Lehmann and Sonia Roccas: 'Multimethod Probes of Basic Human Values', in *Social Psychology and Cultural Context*, ed. John Adamopoulos and Yoshihisa Kashima (Sage, 1999).

[7] Schwartz et al.: 'Extending the Cross-Cultural Validity of the Theory of Basic Human Values with a Different Method of Measurement.'

[8] Schwartz continues to test and perfect the scale.

[9] Schwartz et al.: 'Extending the Cross-Cultural Validity of the Theory of Basic Human Values with a Different Method of Measurement.'

[10] See Richard W. Brislin, Walter J. Lonner and Robert M. Thorndike: *Cross-Cultural Research Methods*, ed. Robert T. Holt and John E. Turner, *Comparative Studies in Behavioral Science* (Wiley, 1973).

[11] Schwartz et al.: 'Extending the Cross-Cultural Validity of the Theory of Basic Human Values with a Different Method of Measurement'; Schwartz, Lehmann and Roccas: 'Multimethod Probes of Basic Human Values.'

[12] For more details on the analysis and weighting, see Schwartz: 'Universals in the Content and Structure of Values: Theoretical Advances and Empirical Tests in 20 Countries.'

[13] ibid.

[14] Burgess and Harris: 'Values, Optimum Stimulation Levels and Brand Loyalty: New Scales in New Populations'; Burgess and Steenkamp: 'Value Priorities and Consumer Behavior in a Transitional Economy: The Case of South Africa'; Schwartz et al.: 'Extending the Cross-Cultural Validity of the Theory of Basic Human Values with a Different Method of Measurement.'

[15] A Ward's Method minimum variance cluster analysis was performed and the scree plot was examined to determine the best possible number of clusters following the procedure used by Steven M. Burgess and Mari Harris: 'Social Identity in an Emerging Consumer Market: How You Do the Wash May Say a Lot About Who You Think You Are', *Advances in Consumer Research* 26 (1999). The final clusters were determined using k-means cluster analysis for the suggested 16-cluster solution.

[16] Intermarket segments are groups of people who represent coherent groups with consistent behaviour patterns across markets. For instance, people in the southern suburbs of Cape Town and the northern suburbs of Durban, Johannesburg and Harare represent highly educated populations with global outlook. These groups share much in common and may act similarly in response to promotional communications, product and pricing strategies.

Chapter 5

[1] The difference is significant at $p<.001$. Remembering that we have randomly selected South Africans who we hope are representative of all South Africans, we can be confident that the groups will differ at least 999 out of 1000 times given the results we achieved – a high level of confidence indeed!

[2] Roger D. Blackwell, Paul W. Miniard and James F. Engel: *Consumer Behavior*, 10th ed. (Harcourt, 2000).

[3] ibid.

[4] Burgess and Harris: 'Social Identity in an Emerging Consumer Market: How You Do the Wash May Say a Lot About Who You Think You Are.'

⁵ Gordon V. Kass: 'An Exploratory Technique for Investigating Large Quantities of Categorical Data', *Applied Statistics* 29 (1980).

⁶ Burgess and Harris: 'Social Identity in an Emerging Consumer Market: How You Do the Wash May Say a Lot About Who You Think You Are.'

⁷ Burgess and Harris argued that these results could be explained by the link between the country-of-origin associated with the brand image and the social identity of the SA Tribe. They predicted that 'clusters' 3, 8, 11 and 12 would be more likely to use brands that had a strong European or American identity associated with the brand through advertising.

Chapter 6

¹ See Robert Mattes: 'Hypotheses on Identity and Democracy: Community, Regime, Institutions and Citizenship', in *Identity, Politics and History*, ed. Simon Bekker and Rachel Prinsloo (Human Sciences Research Council, 1999).

² The sample sizes were Botswana = 1,200, Lesotho = 1,177, Malawi = 1,208, Mali = 1,200, Namibia = 1,183, Nigeria = 3,603, South Africa = 2,200, Tanzania = 2,200, Zambia = 1,200 and Zimbabwe = 1,200.

³ Samples were drawn using a common clustered, stratified, multi-stage area probability design. Random selection methods were used at each stage, with probability according to population size wherever possible. Sampling frames were constructed in the first stages from the most up-to-data census data or projections available, and thereafter from census maps, systematic walk patterns and project-generated lists of household members. With the exception of South Africa, each country sample was self-weighted and sufficiently representative of national characteristics on key socio-economic indicators (age, gender, region) that post-weighting was not necessary.

⁴ A similar conclusion is reached by Gabriel Almond: *A Discipline Divided: Schools and Sects in Political Science* (Sage, 1990).

⁵ Walker Connor: 'Ethnonationalism and Political Instability', in *The Exclusive Search for Peace: Israel, South Africa and Northern Ireland*, ed. J. Gagiano and H. Giliomee (Oxford University Press, 1990); Arend Lijphart: *Democracy in Plural Societies: A Comparative Exploration* (Yale University Press, 1977).

⁶ Connor: 'Ethnonationalism and Political Instability.'

⁷ Juan Linz and Alfred Stepan: 'Toward Consolidated Democracies', *Journal of Democracy* 7, no. 2 (1996).

⁸ Ernst Gellner: *Nations and Nationalism* (Blackwell, 1983). Also see David Manent: 'Democracy without Nations', *Journal of Democracy* 8, no. 2 (1997); Dankwart Rustow: 'Democracy: A Global Revolution', *Foreign Affairs* (1990); Dankwart Rustow: 'Transition to Democracy: Toward a Dynamic Model', *Comparative Politics* 2 (1970).

⁹ Connor: 'Ethnonationalism and Political Instability'; Johan Degenaar: 'Beware of Nation-Building Discourse', in *Democratic Nation-Building in South Africa*, ed. Nic Rhoodie and Ian Liebenberg (Human Sciences Research Council, 1994).

[10] Robert Mattes: 'Do Diverse Social Identities Inhibit Nationhood and Democracy?', in *National Identity and Democracy in Africa*, ed. Mai Palmbert (Human Sciences Research Council, 1999 – also Mayibuye Centre at the University of the Western Cape and the Nordic Africa Institute). Also see the various papers in Nic Rhoodie and Ian Liebenberg, eds.: *Democratic Nation-Building in South Africa* (Human Sciences Research Council, 1994).

[11] Heribert Adam: 'Nationalism, Nation-Building and Non-Racialism', in *Democratic Nation-Building in South Africa*, ed. Nic Rhoodie and Ian Liebenberg (Human Sciences Research Council, 1994).

[12] For example, David Horowitz: *A Democratic South Africa? Constitutional Engineering in a Divided Society* (Oxford University Press, 1991).

[13] Like SA Tribes, Tajfel's work on social identity also informed our approach to defining identity. For more information on social identity and social categorisation theory, see Chapter 2 in this book and the references cited there.

[14] The underlying questions differ somewhat from year to year. For 1994 and 1995, Idasa asked: 'In terms of culture, history and language, do you belong to a distinctive community (with its own distinctive culture and history)? IF YES: To which community do you belong? IF NO: How would you describe yourselves in one or two words?' In 1997, Idasa asked: 'We have spoken to many people and they have all described themselves in different ways. Some people describe themselves in terms of their language, for example Swazi, Zulu or Sotho. Other people describe themselves according to their religion such as Methodist or Jewish. Still other people describe themselves in terms of their race, for example Asian or black, and some people describe themselves as working class, middle class or upper class. Thinking about yourself, which specific group do you feel you belong to first and foremost?' In 2000, Afrobarometer asked: 'We have spoken to many South Africans and they have all described themselves in different ways. Some people describe themselves in terms of their language, religion, race, and others describe themselves in economic terms, such as working class, middle class or a farmer. Besides being South African, to which specific group do you feel you belong to first and foremost?'

[15] Horowitz: *A Democratic South Africa? Constitutional Engineering in a Divided Society*.

[16] Future researchers may well help us understand the answers to such questions, for instance by including a well-documented social desirability response bias scale in their research, such as the Marlowe-Crowne scale. See, for instance, Douglas P. Crowne and David Marlowe: 'A New Scale of Social Desirability Independent of Psychopathology', *Journal of Consulting Psychology* 24, no. 4 (1959).

[17] See, for example, Mattes: 'Do Diverse Social Identities Inhibit Nationhood and Democracy?' Also see the forthcoming book by Michael Bratton and Robert Mattes: *Waiting for Deliverance: People, Democracy and Markets in Africa* (2002).

[18] David Welsh: 'The Making of the Constitution', in *The Bold Experiment: South Africa's New Democracy*, ed. Herman Giliomee, Lawrence Schlemmer and Sarita Hauptflesh (Southern Books, 1994).

Chapter 7

[1] See, for example, A. J. Christopher: 'Urban Segregation Levels in South Africa under Apartheid', *Sociology and Social Research* 75, no. 1 (1991); L. Human and M. J. Greenacre: 'Labour Market Discrimination in the Manufacturing Sector: The Impact of Race, Gender, Education and Age on Income', *The South African Journal of Economics* 55, no. 2 (1987); Main Committee: HSRC Investigation into Intergroup Relations; *The South African Society: Realities and Future Prospects* (Human Sciences Research Council, 1985).

[2] Batra: 'Marketing Issues and Challenges in Transitional Economies.'

Chapter 8

[1] See Burgess (1998) for a discussion of consumer behaviour and extended references.

[2] If you feel uncomfortable identifying a qualified research company, contact the Southern African Marketing Research Association (SAMRA) in Johannesburg. SAMRA maintains a register of qualified members nationally and has a strong ethical code of conduct that regulates their behaviour.

[3] There is a much more rigorous discussion of consumer behaviour issues in Burgess (1998).

[4] See Burgess (1998).

Bibliography

Adam, Heribert. 'Nationalism, Nation-Building and Non-Racialism.' *Democratic Nation-Building in South Africa*, edited by Nic Rhoodie and Ian Liebenberg. Human Sciences Research Council, Pretoria, South Africa, 1994.
Allen, Richard L., Michael C. Dawson and Ronald E. Brown. 'A Schema-Based Approach to Modeling an African-American Racial Belief System.' *American Political Science Review* 83, no. 2 (1989), 421–41.
Allport, G. W. and H. S. Odbert. 'Trait Names: A Psycho-Lexical Study.' *Psychological Monograms* 47, no. 1 (1936).
Almond, Gabriel. *A Discipline Divided: Schools and Sects in Political Science*. Sage, London, 1990.
Batra, Rajeev. 'Marketing Issues and Challenges in Transitional Economies.' *Marketing Issues in Transitional Economies*, edited by Rajeev Batra, 3–35. Kluwer Academic Press, Norwell, Mass., USA, 1999.
Baumgartner, Hans and Jan-Benedict E. M. Steenkamp. 'Multi-Group Latent Variable Models for Varying Numbers of Items and Factors with Cross-National and Longitudinal Applications.' *Marketing Letters* 9, no. 1 (1998): 21–35.
Baumgartner, Hans and Jan-Benedict E. M. Steenkamp. 'Exploratory Consumer Behaviour: Conceptualization and Measurement.' *International Journal of Research in Marketing* 13, no. 2 (1996): 121–37.
Biernat, Monica, Theresa K. Vescio, Shelley A. Theno and Christian S. Crandall. 'Values and Prejudice: Toward Understanding the Impact of American Values on Outgroup Attitudes.' *The Psychology of Values: The Ontario Symposium*, edited by Clive Seligman, James M. Olson and Mark P. Zanna, 153–90. Lawrence Erlbaum, Hillsdale, New Jersey, USA, 1996.
Blackwell, Roger D., Paul W. Miniard and James F. Engel. *Consumer Behavior*. 10th ed. Harcourt, Fort Worth, Texas, USA, 2000.
Blascovich, Jim, Natalie A. Wyer, Laura A. Swart and Jeffrey L. Kibler. 'Racism and Racial Categorization.' *Journal of Personality and Social Psychology* 72, no. 6 (1997): 1364–72.
Bratton, Michael and Robert Mattes. *Waiting for Deliverance: People, Democracy and Markets in Africa*, 2002.
Brewer, Marilynn B. and Rupert J. Brown. 'Intergroup Relations.' In *The Handbook of Social Psychology*, edited by Daniel T. Gilbert, Susan T. Fiske and Gardner Lindzey, 554–94. McGraw-Hill, Boston, Mass., USA, 1998.
Brewer, Marilynn B. 'In-group Bias in the Minimal Intergroup Situation: A Cognitive-Motivational Analysis.' *Psychological Bulletin* 86 (1979): 307–24.
Brewer, Marilynn B. and Wendi L. Gardner. 'Who Is This 'We'? Levels of Collective Identity and Self-Representations.' *Journal of Personality and Social Psychology* 71 (1996): 83–93.

Brislin, Richard W., Walter J. Lonner and Robert M. Thorndike. *Cross-Cultural Research Methods.* Edited by Robert T. Holt and John E. Turner, *Comparative Studies in Behavioral Science.* Wiley, New York, USA, 1973.

Broman, Clifford L., Harold W. Neighbors and James S. Jackson. 'Racial Group Identification Among Black Adults.' *Social Forces* 67, no. 1 (1988): 146–58.

Burgess, Steven M. *The New Marketing: Building Strong Marketing Strategies in South Africa Today.* Zebra Press – A division of New Holland Struik Publishing Group (Pty) Ltd, Johannesburg, South Africa, 1998.

Burgess, Steven M. 'Personal Values and Consumer Research: An Historical Perspective.' In *Research in Marketing*, edited by Jagdish N. Sheth, 35–79. JAI Press, Greenwich, Connecticut, USA, 1992.

Burgess, Steven M. and Roger D. Blackwell. 'Evaluations of Non-celebrities in Print Ads: An Exploratory Study on the Influence of Source Attractiveness, Similarity and Consumer Values.' Graduate School of Business Working Paper Series, University of Cape Town, Cape Town, South Africa, 2000.

Burgess, Steven M. and Mari Harris. 'High and Low Optimum Stimulation Level Consumers: Their Characteristics, Living Standards, Lifestyle Interests, and Product Choice Behaviors.' Paper presented at the 1998 Academy of Marketing Science Multicultural Marketing Conference, Montreal, Canada, 1998.

Burgess, Steven M. and Mari Harris. 'Social Identity in an Emerging Consumer Market: How You Do the Wash May Say a Lot About Who You Think You Are.' *Advances in Consumer Research* 26 (1999): 170–75.

Burgess, Steven M. and Mari Harris. 'Values, Optimum Stimulation Levels and Brand Loyalty: New Scales in New Populations.' *South African Journal of Business Management* 29, no. 4 (1998): 142–57.

Burgess, Steven M., Shalom H. Schwartz and Roger D. Blackwell. 'Do Values Share Universal Content and Structure? A South African Test.' *South African Journal of Psychology* 24, no. 1 (1994): 1–12.

Burgess, Steven M. and Jan-Benedict E. M. Steenkamp. 'Value Priorities and Consumer Behavior in a Transitional Economy: The Case of South Africa.' *Marketing Issues in Transitional Economies*, edited by Rajeev Batra, 85–105. Kluwer Academic Press, Norwell, Mass., USA, 1999.

Camilleri, Carmel and Hanna Malewska-Peyre. 'Socialization and Identity Strategies.' *Handbook of Cross-Cultural Psychology*, edited by John W. Berry, Pierre R. Dasen and T. S. Saraswati, 41–68. Allyn and Bacon, Boston, Mass., USA, 1997.

Christopher, A. J. 'Urban Segregation Levels in South Africa under Apartheid.' *Sociology and Social Research* 75, no. 1 (1991): 89–94.

Cialdini, R. B., C. A. Kallgren and R. R. Reno. 'A Focus Theory on Normative Conduct: A Theoretical Refinement and Reevaluation of the Role of Norms in Human Behavior.' *Advances in Experimental Social Psychology* 21 (1991): 201–34.

Clinton, Bill. 'The Struggle for the Soul of the 21st Century.' Paper presented at the Dimbleby Lecture 2001, London, 14 December 2001.

Connor, Walker. 'Ethnonationalism and Political Instability.' *The Exclusive Search for Peace: Israel, South Africa and Northern Ireland*, edited by J. Gagiano and H. Giliomee. Oxford University Press, Cape Town, South Africa, 1990.

Crowne, Douglas P. and David Marlowe. 'A New Scale of Social Desirability Independent of Psychopathology.' *Journal of Consulting Psychology* 24, no. 4 (1959): 349–54.

Degenaar, Johan. 'Beware of Nation-Building Discourse.' *Democratic Nation-Building in South Africa*, edited by Nic Rhoodie and Ian Liebenberg. Human Sciences Research Council, Pretoria, South Africa, 1994.

Devine, P.G. 'Stereotypes and Prejudice: Their Automatic and Controlled Components.' *Journal of Personality and Social Psychology* 56 (1989): 5–18.

Ebstein, R. P., L. Nemanov, I. Klotz, I. Gritsenko and R. H. Belmaker. 'Additional Evidence for an Association between the Dopamine D4 Receptor (D4dr) Exon Iii Repeat Polymorphism and the Human Personality Trait of Novelty Seeking.' *Molecular Psychiatry* 2, no. 6 (1997): 472–77.

Ebstein, R. P., O. Novick, R. Umansky, B. Priel, Y. Osher, D. Blaine, E. R. Bennett, E. Nemanov, M. Katz and R. H. Belmaker. 'Dopamine D4 Receptor (D4dr) Exon Iii Polymorphism Associated with the Human Personality Trait of Novelty Seeking.' *Nature Genetics* 12 (1996): 78–80.

Fein, Steven and Steven J. Spencer. 'Prejudice as Self-Image Maintenance: Affirming the Self through Derogating Others.' *Social Psychology* 73, no. 1 (1997): 31–44.

Fiske, Susan T. 'Stereotyping, Prejudice, and Discrimination.' *The Handbook of Social Psychology*, edited by Daniel T. Gilbert, Susan T. Fiske and Gardner Lindzey, 357–413. McGraw-Hill, New York, USA, 1998.

Frankl, Victor E. *The Doctor and the Soul*. Knopf, New York, USA, 1955.

Frankl, Victor E. *Man's Search for Meaning*. Beacon, Boston, Mass., USA, 1959.

Garlington, W. K. and H. E. Shimota. 'The Change Seeker Index: A Measure of the Need for Variable Stimulus Input.' *Psychological Reports* 14 (1964): 919–24.

Gellner, Ernst. *Nations and Nationalism*. Basil Blackwell, Oxford, UK, 1983.

Gudykunst, William B. and Michael Harris Bond. 'Intergroup Relations across Cultures.' In *Handbook of Cross-Cultural Psychology*, edited by John W. Berry, Marshall H. Segall and Cigdem Kagitçibasi, 119–62. Allyn and Bacon, Boston, Mass., USA, 1997.

Higgins, E. Tory. 'The 'Self Digest': Self-Knowledge Serving Self-Regulatory Functions.' *Journal of Personality and Social Psychology* 71, no. 6 (1996): 1062–83.

Hogg, M. and D. Abrams. *Social Identifications*. Routledge, London, UK, 1988.

Hooper, Michael. 'The Structure and Measurement of Social Identity.' *Public Opinion Quarterly* 40, no. 2 (1976): 154–64.

Horowitz, David. *A Democratic South Africa? Constitutional Engineering in a Divided Society*. Oxford University Press, Cape Town, South Africa, 1991.

Human, L. and M. J. Greenacre. 'Labour Market Discrimination in the Manufacturing Sector: The Impact of Race, Gender, Education and Age on Income.' *The South African Journal of Economics* 55, no. 2 (1987): 150–64.

Jackson, Linda A., Linda A. Sullivan, Richard Harnish and Carol N. Hodge. 'Achieving Positive Social Identity: Social Mobility, Social Creativity and Permeability of Group Boundaries.' *Journal of Personality and Social Psychology* 70, no. 2 (1996): 241–54.

Kass, Gordon V. 'An Exploratory Technique for Investigating Large Quantities of Categorical Data.' *Applied Statistics* 29 (1980): 119–27.

Kelly, George A. *A Theory of Personality: The Psychology of Personal Constructs*. Norton, New York, USA, 1950.

Lastovicka, John L. 'On the Validation of Lifestyle Traits: A Review and Illustration.' *Journal of Marketing Research* 19, no. 1 (1982): 126–38.

Lijphart, Arend. *Democracy in Plural Societies: A Comparative Exploration*. Yale University Press, New Haven, USA, 1977.

Linz, Juan and Alfred Stepan. 'Toward Consolidated Democracies.' *Journal of Democracy* 7, no. 2 (1996).
Main Committee: HSRC Investigation into Intergroup Relations. *The South African Society: Realities and Future Prospects*. Human Sciences Research Council, Pretoria, South Africa, 1985.
Manent, David. 'Democracy without Nations.' *Journal of Democracy* 8, no. 2 (1997).
Markus, H. 'Self-Schemata and Processing Information About the Self.' *Journal of Personality and Social Psychology* 35, no. 1 (1977): 63–78.
Mattes, Robert. 'Do Diverse Social Identities Inhibit Nationhood and Democracy?' In *National Identity and Democracy in Africa*, edited by Mai Palmbert, 268–71. Human Sciences Research Council, Pretoria, South Africa (also Mayibuye Centre at the University of the Western Cape and the Nordic Africa Institute), 1999.
Mattes, Robert. 'Hypotheses on Identity and Democracy: Community, Regime, Institutions and Citizenship.' In *Identity, Politics and History*, edited by Simon Bekker and Rachel Prinsloo. Human Sciences Research Council, Pretoria, South Africa, 1999.
McCrae, Robert R. 'Trait Psychology and the Revival of Personality and Culture Studies.' *American Behavioral Scientist* 44, no. 1 (2000): 10–31.
Mead, George Herbert. *Mind, Self and Society*. Chicago: University of Chicago Press, 1934.
Monroe, Kent B. 'Editorial.' *Journal of Consumer Research* 19, no. March (1993).
Quelch, John A. and James E. Austin. 'Should Multinationals Invest in Africa?' *Sloan Management Review*, no. Spring (1993): 107–19.
Raju, P. S. 'Optimum Stimulation Level: Its Relationship to Personality, Demographics, and Exploratory Behavior.' *Journal of Consumer Research* 7, no. December (1980): 272–82.
Rhoodie, Nic and Ian Liebenberg, eds. *Democratic Nation-Building in South Africa*. Human Sciences Research Council, Pretoria, South Africa, 1994.
Rogers, Carl R. *On Becoming a Person: A Therapist's View of Psychotherapy*. Constable, London, UK, 1967.
Rogers, Everitt. *Diffusion of Innovations*. The Free Press, New York, USA, 1962.
Rokeach, Milton. 'Inducing Change and Stability in Belief Systems and Personality Structures.' *Journal of Social Issues* 41, no. 1 (1985): 153–71.
Rokeach, Milton. *The Nature of Human Values*. The Free Press, New York, USA, 1973.
Rokeach, Milton. *Understanding Human Values*. The Free Press, New York, USA, 1979.
Rosenberg, Morris. *Conceiving the Self*. Basic Books, New York, USA, 1979.
Rustow, Dankwart. 'Democracy: A Global Revolution.' *Foreign Affairs* (1990).
Rustow, Dankwart. 'Transition to Democracy: Toward a Dynamic Model.' *Comparative Politics* 2 (1970).
Schwartz, Shalom. 'Universals in the Content and Structure of Values: Theoretical Advances and Empirical Tests in 20 Countries.' *Advances in Experimental Social Psychology* 25 (1992): 1–49.
Schwartz, Shalom H. 'Are There Universal Aspects in the Content and Structure of Human Values?' *Journal of Social Issues* 50, no. 4 (1994): 19–45.
Schwartz, Shalom H. 'Normative Influence on Altruism.' In *Advances in Experimental Social Psychology*, edited by L. Berkowitz, 221–79. Academic Press, New York, USA, 1977.

Schwartz, Shalom H., Arielle Lehmann, Gila Melech, Steven M. Burgess, Mari Harris and Vicki Owens. 'Extending the Cross-Cultural Validity of the Theory of Basic Human Values with a Different Method of Measurement.' *Journal of Cross-Cultural Psychology* 32, no. 5 (2001): 519–42.

Schwartz, Shalom H., Arielle Lehmann and Sonia Roccas. 'Multimethod Probes of Basic Human Values.' In *Social Psychology and Cultural Context*, edited by John Adamopoulos and Yoshihisa Kashima, 107–23. Sage, Newbury Park, Calif., USA, 1999.

Schwartz, Shalom H. and Maria Ros. 'Values in the West: A Theoretical and Empirical Challenge to the Individualism-Collectivism Cultural Dimension.' *World Psychology* 1, no. 2 (1995): 91–122.

Sherif, Muzafer. *Group Conflict and Co-Operation: Their Social Psychology*. Routledge and Kegan Paul, London, UK, 1966.

Sherif, Muzafer. *The Psychology of Social Norms*. Harper Row, New York, USA, 1936.

Steenkamp, Jan-Benedict E. M., Frankel ter Hofstede and Michel Wedel. 'A Cross-National Investigation into the Individual and Cultural Antecedents of Consumer Innovativeness.' *Journal of Marketing Research* 36, no. February (1999): 1–17.

Steenkamp, Jan-Benedict E. M. and Hans Baumgartner. 'Development and Cross-Cultural Validation of a Short Form Csi as a Measure of Optimum Stimulation Level.' *International Journal of Research in Marketing* 12, no. 2 (1995): 97–104.

Steenkamp, Jan-Benedict E. M. and Hans Baumgartner. 'The Role of Optimum Stimulation Level in Exploratory Consumer Behavior.' *Journal of Consumer Research* 19, no. December (1992): 434–48.

Steenkamp, Jan-Benedict E. M. and Steven M. Burgess. 'Optimum Stimulation Level and Exploratory Consumer Behaviour in an Emerging Consumer Market.' *International Journal of Research in Marketing* 19 (2002).

Steenkamp, Jan-Benedict E. M., Hans Baumgartner and Elise Van der Wulp. 'Arousal Potential, Arousal, Stimulus Attractiveness, and the Moderating Role of Need for Stimulation.' *International Journal of Research in Marketing* 13, no. 4 (1996): 319–29.

Struch, Naomi and Shalom H. Schwartz. 'Intergroup Aggression: Its Predictors and Distinctness from In-group Bias.' *Journal of Personality and Social Psychology* 56, no. 3 (1989): 364–73.

Sumner, William Graham. *Folkways*. Ginn, New York, USA, 1906.

Sussman, Nan M. 'The Dynamic Nature of Cultural Identity Throughout Cultural Transitions: Why Home Is Not So Sweet.' *Personality and Social Psychology Review* 4, no. 4 (2000): 355–73.

Tajfel, Henri. *Differentiation between Social Groups: Studies in the Social Psychology of Intergroup Relations*. Academic Press, London, UK, 1978.

Tajfel, Henri. 'Experiments in Intergroup Discrimination.' *Scientific American* 223, no. 2 (1970): 96–102.

Tajfel, Henri. *Human Groups and Social Categories: Studies in Social Psychology*. Cambridge University Press, Cambridge, UK, 1981.

Tajfel, Henri. 'Social Identity and Intergroup Behavior.' *Social Science Information* 13, no. 2 (1974): 65–93.

Tajfel, Henri, ed. *The Social Dimension: European Studies in Social Psychology*. 2 vols. Cambridge University Press, Cambridge, UK, 1984.

Tajfel, Henri and J. C. Turner. 'An Integrative Theory of Intergroup Conflict.' In *The Social Psychology of Intergroup Relations*, edited by W. G. Austin and S. Worchel, 33–47. Brooks/Cole, Monterey, Calif., USA, 1979.
Triandis, Harry C. *Individualism and Collectivism*. Westview Press, Boulder, Colorado, USA, 1995.
Triandis, Harry C., Robert Bontempo, Hector Betancourt, Michael Bond, Kwok Leung, Abelando Brenes, James Georgas, C. Harry Hui, Gerardo Marin, Bernadette Setiadi, Jai B. P. Sinha, Jyoti Verma, John Spangenberg, Hubert Touzard and Germaine de Montmollin. 'The Measurement of the Etic Aspects of Individualism and Collectivism across Cultures.' *Australian Journal of Psychology* 38, no. 3 (1986): 257–67.
Triandis, Harry C., Kwok Leung, M. J. Villareal and F. L. Clack. 'Allocentric Versus Idiocentric Tendencies: Convergent and Discriminant Validation.' *Journal of Research in Personality* 19 (1985): 395–415.
Triandis, Harry C., Christopher McCusker and C. Harry Hui. 'Multimethod Probes of Individualism and Collectivism.' *Journal of Personality and Social Psychology* 59, no. November (1990): 1006–20.
Tyson, G. A., Anne Schlachter and Saths Cooper. 'Game Playing Strategy as an Indicator of Racial Prejudice among South African Students.' *The Journal of Social Psychology* 128, no. 4 (1987): 473–85.
United Nations Development Programme. 'Human Development Report 2000: Human Rights and Human Development.' 290. Oxford University Press, New York, USA, 2000.
Vaughan, Graham M. 'Social Change and Racial Identity: Issues in the Use of Picture and Doll Measures.' *Australian Journal of Psychology* 38, no. 3 (1986): 359–70.
Verkuyten, Maykel and Louk Hagendoorn. 'Prejudice and Self-Categorization: The Variable Role of Authoritarianism and In-Group Stereotypes.' *Personality and Social Psychology Bulletin* 24, no. 1 (1998): 99–110.
Vinson, Donald E., Jerome Scott, E. and Lawrence M. Lamont. 'The Role of Personal Values in Marketing and Consumer Behavior.' *Journal of Marketing*, no. April (1977): 44–50.
Welsh, David. 'The Making of the Constitution.' In *The Bold Experiment: South Africa's New Democracy*, edited by Herman Giliomee, Lawrence Schlemmer and Sarita Hauptflesh. Halfway House: Southern Books, 1994.
Winter, David G., Oliver P. John, Abigail J. Stewart, Eva C. Klohnen and Lauren E. Duncan. 'Traits and Motives: Toward an Integration of Two Traditions in Personality Research.' *Psychological Review* 105, no. 2 (1998): 230–50.
Zegeye, Abebe. 'Imposed Ethnicity.' In *Social Identities in the New South Africa*, edited by Abebe Zegeye. Kwela Books, Cape Town, South Africa, 2001.
Zuckerman, Marvin. *Behavioral Expressions and Biosocial Bases of Sensation Seeking*. Cambridge University Press, Cambridge, UK, 1994.
Zuckerman, Marvin. *Sensation Seeking: Beyond the Optimal Level of Arousal*. Lawrence Erlbaum, Hinsdale, New Jersey, USA, 1979.

Index

Page numbers in *italics* indicate figures or tables.

Achievers group 66–67, 73
Agrarian Lifestyles 51–52, 72
All Media and Products Survey (AMPS)
    23, 39, 43
Apartheid legacy 5, 12, 19, 23, 35, 84, 85
attitudes 27

benevolence 26, 28
bias, in-group 16–18
books (fiction) 70–71, *71*
Border Survivalists 52–53
brand choice, and identity 75–81,
    76–77, 80
business
    identity within firm 117
    and market orientation 114–115, *114*
    problem recognition 115–116
    providing solutions 116
    purchase and outcomes 117

Cape Coloured Emerging 59, 72
    and political issues 99, 101, 103, 104,
        107, 112
categorical attributes 23
categorisation 20–22
CDs 71–72, *71*
central dispositions 26–27
CHAID analysis 77–78
Change Seeker Index (CSI) 40, 125n5
clothing (women) 72–73, *73*
cluster analysis 47, 126n15
collectivism, and individualism 32–33
consumer behaviour, and value priorities
    30–31
corruption 104–107, *106*
courtesy bias 41, 123n36
CSI *see* Change Seeker Index
culture, and values 31–33

demographic characteristics 4, 19, 39
digest of selves 6

Earth Mothers group 64–65
East Coast Settlers 60–61
Emerging Consumers 49, 68, 71
    Cape Coloured Emerging 59
    Free State Emerging 56–57
    Gauteng Township Youth 58
    Matchbox Suburban Youth 57–58
    and political issues 99–100, 101, 102,
        103, 104, 106, 107, 112
    Prime Skills 59–60
emerging economies 7–8, 36, 104
ethnicity 92, 93
exploratory consumer behaviours 25

Family Focus group 65–66, 72, 111
Frankl, Victor 25–26, 123n37
Free State Emerging 56–57, 112

gardening 73–74
Gauteng Township Youth 58
government, and implications of
    identity 117–119
group chauvinism 88, 89, *89*, 94
group identity 12, 88–89, *88*, 118

health 72, *72*, 104, *105*
Highveld Survivalists 53–54, 112
HIV/AIDS 14, 104
housing 102–103, *102*, *103*

Idasa 82, 84–85, 128n14
identity 1–2, 10–11, 33–34
    see also social identity
    and brand choice 75–81, *76–77, 80*
    and cultural differences 31–33

INDEX

and future of South Africa 117–119
and lifestyle interests 70–74, *71*, *72*, *73*, *74*
model of identity influence *38*, *114*
personal identity 11
relational identity 11
within firm 117
identity components 22–23
  categorical attributes 23
  personality traits 4, 19, 24–25
individualism, and collectivism 32–33
individuals, and national identity 119
inflation 99–101, *100*
in-group bias 16–18
injunctive norms 32
Institute for Democracy in South Africa *see* Idasa
intergroup behaviour 13, 16–18
  awareness of differentiated group 18–19
  behavioural differences 19
  in-group bias 16–18
  perceived similarity 19
intermarket segments 50, 126n16

KZN Survivalists 55, 106, 107, 110, 111, 112

lifestyle 26–27, 40
and identity 70–74, *71*, *72*, *73*, *74*
living standard measure (LSM) 39, 40

market orientation 114–115, *114*
Markinor 4, 36, 42–43
Matchbox Suburban Youth 57–58
meaning 26
minimal intergroup situation paradigm 16
motivational values 28–30, *29*, 30–31
multiple correspondence analysis *46*, 47

national identity 89–91, *90*, *91*, 92–93, 94–96, 118, 119
nation building 91, 96–97
norms 32

observable characteristics 4, 19, 39
optimum stimulation level (OSL) 24–25, 40, *42*, 123n32
personal identity 11, 14
personality traits 4, 19, 24–25, 26
personal norms 32
political attitudes 98–99
  and political party support 107, *108–109*
  towards corruption in government 104–107, *106*
  towards government's management of economy 101–102, *101*
  towards health 104, *105*
  towards housing 102–103, *102*, *103*
  towards inflation 99–101, *100*
  towards personal circumstances 107, 110–112, *110*, *111*
political party support 107, *108–109*
politics, and social identity 82–83
Portrait Values Questionnaire (PVQ) 41, 42
prejudice 22
Prime Skills group 59–60, 107, 110
problem recognition 115–116

race 19, 35, 92
racial identity 5–6, 12, 22, 85, 88
records 71–72, *71*
regression analyses 78
relational identity 11, 14
response bias 45–47
Rokeach, Milton 27
Rural Survivalists 48–49, 67, 72, 73, 75, 116
  Agrarian Lifestyles 51–52
  Border Survivalists 52–53
  Highveld Survivalists 53–54
  KZN Survivalists 55
  and political issues 99, 102, 103, 104, 107, 112

schemas 11, 20–22
Schwartz, Shalom 36
  Schwartz Value Survey 41–42
  theory re human values 27–29, *28*, *29*, 33

secondary dispositions 26–27
social conflict 15
social creativity 15
social identity 4–6, 12
  see also identity
  and emerging economies 7–8
  and perceptions 20–21
  and politics 82–83
  role in South Africa 12–13
  and transitional societies 8
social identity and politics 82–83
  importance 83–84
  in South Africa 84–93, *86*, *87*, *88*, *89*, *90*, *91*, *92*
  within Africa 93–97, *94*, *95*, *96*, *97*
social identity theory 13–14
  advantages 6–7
  in-group bias 16–18
  positive social identity 15
social mobility 15
South Africa
  as emerging economy & transitional society 8
  influence of categorical attributes 23
  influence of OSL on behaviour 25
  role of social identity 12–13
  social identity and politics 84–93, *86*, *87*, *88*, *89*, *90*, *91*, *92*
South African Advertising Research Foundation (SAARF) 39
subjective norms 32
Suburban Bliss group 62–63, 74
Suburban Challenge group 63–64

Tajfel, Henri 4
  intergroup behaviour 16–17, 18
  and social identity theory 13–14
  tapes 71–72, *71*

The Believers 61–62, 110, 111, 112
tradition 26, 28
transitional societies 8, 36, 104
tribes *see also* Emerging Consumers; Rural Survivalists; Urban Elite; Urban Middle Classes
  identification 37–39, *38*
  characteristics 39–40, *46*, 47–49, *48*
  choice of sample 42–47, *43*, *44*, *45*
  four groupings *46*, 47–49, *48*
  model of identity influence *38*, *114*
  values 41–42, *42*
  worldview and needs 67–69

ubuntu 32
Urban Elite 49, 67, 68, 71, 73, 74, 75, 116
  Achievers 66–67
  Earth Mothers 64–65
  Family Focus 65–66
  and political issues 99–100, 103, 104, 106, 107
Urban Middle Class 49, 68, 107
  East Coast Settlers 60–61
  Suburban Bliss 62–63
  Suburban Challenge 63–64
  The Believers 61–62

values 4, 19, 25–27
  and culture 31–33
  Portrait Values Questionnaire (PVQ) 41, 42
  scale use bias 123n36
  Schwartz theory 27–29, *28*, *29*
  Schwartz Value Survey 41–42
  value priorities 30–31, *42*

Welsh, David 96–97